Mindful

Ultramarathon

Running

Train to Run Longer, Stronger and
Faster with Less Effort

By:

Michael D'Aulerio

Mindful Ultramarathon Running

Copyright © 2020 by Michael D'Aulerio

All rights reserved.

For information about this title or to order other books and/or electronic media, contact the publisher:

Long Run Living LLC

longrunliving@gmail.com

http://www.LongRunLiving.com

Printed in the USA

The information presented herein represents the view of the author as of the date of publication. This book is presented for informational purposes only. Due to the rate at which conditions change, the author reserves the right to alter and update his opinions based on new conditions. While every attempt has been made to verify the information in this book, neither the author nor his affiliates/partners assume any responsibility for error, inaccuracies, or omissions.

Disclaimer

Table of Contents

Dear New Running Shoes,

You may not understand what's about to take place. There's a great deal of wear and tear coming your way.

Ups and downs, countless miles, and a whole lot of struggle.

However, I can promise you that if you stick with me . . . in the end . . . when you are completely broken, worn down, and beaten . . . when layer upon layer comes off . . . a funny thing happens.

With less, you will feel more . . .

. . . and you will experience a profound wholeness that you never knew existed, safe and enclosed, back in your original little box.

It's going to be a beautiful struggle of a journey, but a journey worth taking.

Will it be easy? No, every step can be a painful step to the finish. But will it be worth it?

YES, every step of the way . . .

With much love and gratitude,

~The One from Above You, Running with You, Every Step of the Way

PREFACE:

Journey Forward

❝One day I laced up a pair of running shoes to learn how to run; who knew that one day they would teach me how to fly?❞

—Michael D'Aulerio, author

Exceeding your perceived limitations and running an ultramarathon is a life-changing pursuit. It's a uniquely gratifying experience and, at the same time, a mighty stressful one. For this reason, you'll soon learn a new way of running. Instead of avoiding stress that weakens, you'll embrace it to become stronger. This new inner power will allow you to become more enduring by using the pain to transcend limitations and reach farther ultramarathon distances. In other words, you will learn to run longer with less force, that is, with less effort.

That's where mindful ultramarathon running can take you. It will lead you deep into the outer realm of the running world where some of the greatest athletes of all time reside. For these runners, the sky is not the limit. Ultra runners race in the sky. Therefore, the only barriers that exist are self-created in the mind. Soon, if you choose, you will run distances you presently can't conceive possible. Get excited!

Remember, if you continue to discover ways to exceed your limits, outside your comfort zone eventually becomes the new inside and what once seemed difficult is now what you do best. Still, collectively, we struggle with the idea of running beyond the physical. We grapple with this thought because the act of running, on the surface, happens through the body. We perceive it through our senses. We see it with our eyes and hear it with our ears.

For that reason, yes, in its most literal form, running is physical. But literalism lacks meaning, and it's meaning that provides purpose, and a big enough purpose is what fuels your progress in running ultramarathon distances.

At the same time, just as every machine has a computer, every pair of legs has a mind. And just as every computer has a user, every mind has an observer. Therefore, running your first ultramarathon or reaching a farther distance is much more of an inside job than it is an outside one. The journey outward always begins inward.

If you are looking to run incredibly long distances, then you've come to the right place. Whether you are an experienced ultramarathon runner searching for a smoother path or a potential one who is looking to make sense out of the miles, mindful ultramarathon running can be your answer. It has the potential to help you reach farther distances with a smile on your face. Now wouldn't that be an amazing change of events? Sure it would.

So what is mindful ultramarathon running? Well, it's a lot of things for a lot of different people. I'll be delivering this concept in a unique way—a way that's helped me run multiple 100- and 200-mile races. A way that's kept me running nonstop for twenty-four hours in below-freezing temperatures and seventy-two hours in one race. A way that's allowed me to run over one hundred ultra-distances in only a handful of years. And now, I will share my thought process with you in this book, as your guide, while assisting you every step of the way.

First, understand this book, *Mindful Ultramarathon Running*, is not a strategy. Instead, I ask you to see it as a key to unlock your unlimited potential. It's how you'll handle the resistance, pain, and stress that commonly occurs with ultra running and find greater clarity to set you free. You will use the valleys to construct much higher peaks until it becomes a habit.

Soon you will develop the insight to continue moving forward even in your darkest moments. Because it takes entering into a vast darkness to find a radiant light. And no, I'm not referring to your headlamp on a midnight trail. What I'm referring to is your higher self. I'm talking about your invincible human spirit. The spirit that's in you, and that same spirit that's in me.

This book is not a rigid set of rules to follow. Instead, it's a guide to help propel you through barriers and into the inner realm of ultramarathon running. This realm isn't a destination you find outwardly, but a new world that awaits inwardly. Because that's where the real power lies: it's within you.

Soon you will learn to let go of conclusions and beliefs, because these assumptions limit the distance you can run. As far as we know, there's an infinite universe, with limitless potential. We then try to take a few of its scrambled pieces, connect them together, and claim we know how things work. *Mindful Ultramarathon Running* will teach you how to let go of conclusions, because those limiting stories prevent you from running longer. And it's these same stories that your ego clings to, misidentifying itself and leading you off the path of ultramarathon running.

You're not too old; you're not too young. You're not too skinny; you're not too fat. You're not too busy; you're not too lazy. Your life, my friend, is way too meaningful to waste away on the sidelines in wonder, pondering if you could really be the runner you wish you could be. You are a miracle, and any opposition is just fear and conditioning.

So let go and allow the natural flow of life to carry you forward. Do this, and instead of feeling like you're traveling upstream with force, you will flow downstream with grace. You'll find your stride to be smoother while running longer with less effort. How refreshing and relieving the life of a mindful ultramarathon runner can be.

To run mindfully is to run with thought behind it, and since our thoughts are what we become, I will provide you with a new way of thinking for ultramarathon running. A mindset that helps ensure you cross the finish line, every time, whether you're running 50K, 50 miles, 100K, 100 miles, 200 miles, or longer!

With that, are you ready to stop running with your legs and start running with your mind? Are you ready to relax into your long run and find a new rhythm and flow? Are you ready to find comfort within the uncomfortable so you run the longest of distances?

We'll also take your newfound mindfulness and shift it over into your everyday life, where your love for life becomes a reciprocal of the miles you run. Where forms of measurement like time and distance become an abstract illusion and where you find peace in the moment.

If you're anything like me, then you have a sincere love for the distance. It doesn't matter if I'm running down trails, over mountains, through roadways, or on a beach. To run mindfully is to run in the present. The "NOW" is a marvelous place to find an appreciation for the world and all its majestic surroundings.

You see, no matter where you run, when doing so mindfully, not only can you run multiple ultramarathons, you can find longevity in the sport. Trust me when I tell you, I didn't run over one hundred ultramarathon distances because it was an obsessive goal. No, it wasn't some fierce desire for another accomplishment, although it might have started off that way. Instead, running ultramarathon distances simply became a way of my being. I don't mention this to impress you, but instead, to press upon you that it's possible for anyone to run these distances, and that includes you.

You see, how far you run outwardly is merely a reflection of how deep you are willing to dig inwardly, and every step you take inwardly is another step you can take outwardly.

What a divine cause and effect.

I can tell you from experience, whether I'm on a 10-, 100-, or 200-mile run, every step forward is a representation of who I am, and in that sense, who you are. Think about it, movement is the way of life. Consider our vibrational frequency from a subatomic level. Movement

6

is a part of our being. So if moving is who we are, then running is a celebration of life!

Soon you'll realize that if you relax, let go, and have the courage to jump into the unknown, the mileage doesn't just become something you do, it becomes a part of who you are. Even more so, it's where running shifts from a tedious chore to a part of your essence, that is, a part of your soul. Now the miles become an expression of your inner being; they become the notes of your inner vibrational symphony. What a gift running can be.

Over time, you will redirect yourself from being an ultramarathon runner who grinds through race day for satisfaction and relief and become a mindful one who discovers peace and joy in every stride. *Mindful Ultramarathon Running* can take you there.

This book was designed to look at ultramarathon running from a new scope. Together, we are going to strip away thoughts of gear, supplements, races, and other details that make up the smoke screen to your next finish line. You'll focus on something much more important: YOU. The real you. That's the inner you. Not the ego, or the thinker of thought, but the one who observes it all. The one who's eternally patient in the background.

Sure, I'll sprinkle in different training and racing tips for the body. That's natural when discussing ultramarathon running. You'll have to oil the machine, of course. However, this book was written for so much more. Instead of gripping tight on concepts to move forward, you'll let go, and realize that emptiness is actually a wholeness. It's a beautiful freedom that creates an opening for all your dreams to pour in and come true. Dreams like running a 100-mile ultramarathon or longer. In other words, your dreams of a brighter tomorrow.

You see, the natural flow of life is a river of renewal. It's a rhythm. It's death and rebirth. It's up and down. It's here and there. Understanding how to align with this intrinsically and extrinsically gives you the ability to anticipate, maximize, and most importantly, appreciate every moment of every stride. Joy and suffering are maxed out emotions on the same plane. The shift is subtle and completely in your control. You can allow circumstances to dictate how you feel. That is, they can be the effect of some other cause. Or you can be a positive effect on race day that directs every step of your experience.

Remember, what goes up, must come down, and at the same time, what comes down, must go up. As you may know already, you can fall into a deep low on race day where everything inside of you screams to DNF (short for "did not finish"). Well, this book will help you adopt a new mindset to use those DNF moments for traveling higher on the wave that flows to the shore of the finish line. Yes, what goes down will eventually come back up again. If you look closely, there are cycles all around you, whether it's the cycle of the moon or the cycle of your compulsions or the stages of sleep or the seasons of the earth. Recognizing the cycle of life in everything, and not taking it personally, is your first step to becoming a mindful ultramarathon runner.

You have to break down if you want to grow. With the right focus and direction, you can use the down to lift you up higher than ever before. You can't avoid stress, but you can transcend the pain. To struggle through your ultramarathon journey is not a choice, but how long you suffer—and if you grow from it—is your decision undoubtedly.

With that, I'm honored to be your guide in your new journey, an eternal journey, a journey of love, faith, and determination. Of appreciation, courage, and perseverance. Of passion, compassion, and insight. Of creation, positivity, and acceptance. Of light, life, and yes, of running!

If I do my job, by the end of this book, you will no longer want to run the mileage for achieving more. Instead, you will run ultramarathon distances for humanity, for life, for love, and for the ones you care for most. You will no longer push to run. You will be drawn to run on account of your new mindful ultramarathon running practice. Soon the unthinkable becomes thinkable, the impossible becomes possible, and the unreal becomes your reality.

When you take your focus off the mileage and place it on something infinitely larger than who you are or what you are, the ultramarathon distance becomes nothing more than a speck of dirt on the infinite trail of life. It's a piece of gravel in the sand; an atomic particle in the universe. Now that 200-mile race doesn't seem all the difficult, does it? It's only one tiny arrival out of infinite arrivals in your endless journey.

If you're ready to open your mind, tap into your unlimited potential, and find a more balanced and growth-oriented life through ultra running, then come aboard for the ride of your life. It's time to make some new and healthy changes, discover your true inner powers, and run some extraordinarily long distances along the way.

Now, before we dive in, I'd like to take you along the course of my first 200-mile ultramarathon. A place where ultramarathon running, for me, morphed from a physical endeavor to a spiritual journey. Keep reading as we set sail on your new mindful ultramarathon running voyage together.

INTRODUCTION:

The Way

In an article I published with *Ultrarunning* magazine, I write about my experience running 200 miles for the first time. Now, I'd like to deepen the story and share a small part of my journey with you. It begins at the starting line. A place where ultramarathon running transcended from a physical conquest to a personal spiritual journey. It's also where I started to grasp a deeper understanding of the eternal mystery of our being. The paradox of our existence. How we can hold our body-self and spiritual-self together, as the walking contradictions we are. Today, I openly allow this mystery to move me forward to even farther distances, and you can, too, but first, a poem:

"If you're going to try, go all the way.

Otherwise, don't even start.

If you're going to try, go all the way.

This could mean losing girlfriends, wives, relatives, jobs, and maybe even your mind.

It could mean not eating for three or four days.

It could mean freezing on a park bench.

It could mean jail.

It could mean derision, mockery, isolation.

Isolation is the gift.

All the others are a test of your endurance, of how much you really want to do it.

And, you'll do it, despite rejection and the worst odds.

And it will be better than anything else you can imagine.

If you're going to try, go all the way.

There is no other feeling like that.

You will be alone with the gods, and the nights will flame with fire.

DO IT. DO IT. DO IT. All the way.

You will ride life straight to perfect laughter. It's the only good fight there is."

Go All the Way, a poem by the late Charles Bukowski, contained the last words I heard before approaching the starting line. It was my first 200-mile ultramarathon; a nearly unimaginable distance of unfathomable depths.

If you're an ultramarathon runner, then you've likely heard the following saying: "Running 50 miles will change your life, running 100 miles will rewire your brain." But what happens when you run farther? What happens when you run twice as long as the 100-mile distance?

When you run 200 miles, it will not only reshape your mind, it will bend your reality, and that's just what running a 200-mile ultramarathon did for me. It blasted away any sense of limitations I had left in my running as it morphed common forms of measurement like time and distance into an abstract illusion. Because when you master running in the present moment, how could any such concepts exist?

That race day did not begin at the starting line. For me, it started months prior. The preparation was extensive for both body and mind. My training involved multiple days of heading out the door at 1:00 a.m. running 30, 40, 50, and 60 miles. Multiple 50K distances with no food or water. Plus, every day, I practiced prolonged meditation and read books on spirituality, philosophy, and self-transcendence. The point is this: every small piece of the 200-mile training puzzle contributed to the big picture of race day. The big picture of running a direct route straight through the impossible and right on the other side of insanity.

After training was complete, it was time to hit the road. I packed my bags, kissed my family goodbye, and hopped on a plane. As I headed west to reach my new running goal of 200 miles, I became certain of one thing. I was sure I wouldn't give up, no matter what sacrifices I had to endure.

The park where the race took place held a certain degree of beauty. There was an apparent yet unspoken connection between the runners and the nature contained within the limits of the park. The course consisted of one curvy loop on hard cement. All three days were *hot* . . . really hot. The humidity was high, and there was rarely a cloud in the sky. I was told the heat index broke one hundred degrees.

When the gun went off, I began running. I kept my pace slow and steady with the mantra "slow is fast." After twenty-four hours of running, I was feeling good. Well, as good as you can feel after running 100 miles. Everything was going well; however, this was an ultramarathon . . . right? As ultra runners we know it's not about how you perform when everything goes *right*, it's about how you perform when everything goes *wrong*.

Sooner or later my steady pace broke and I began dealing with a problem I had never faced before. Well, at least not in such severity. So, what went wrong during my first 200-mile ultramarathon? Well, it wasn't the nausea that I quickly cured with a reduction of sugar, and it wasn't the chafing that was stopped by my signature baby powder and diaper-rash cream combination. These issues were expected, and from experience, I knew how to manage them effectively.

No, the biggest problem I faced was blistering. Severe blistering caused mainly from spilling a cooler of water on myself. I developed two huge blisters on the bottom of my feet that made every step a painful step for the better half of the second day. It slowed me down quite a bit, and I mean I really slowed.

As I reached a sloth-like pace, I began to wonder if I could continue through such a tortuous experience. But after some blister maintenance and a solid stretch of downtime, I tied my shoes back up to run. There were many miles to go. It was going to be a tough day to the 200-mile finish. Yet, even with the severe blistering, I had faith, and that incremental speck of faith is what propelled me to move forward. Deep down I knew there was something much larger than myself at work. I knew, as we all do, that I'm meant for so much more in this life, and that's all I needed to get moving. That's all I ever needed.

As I started running again, my blisters were now manageable. It was one step at a time. The farther I ran, the more confident in finishing I became. Once the blisters were under control, it was smooth sailing to the finish . . . right? Far from it. The intense sun exposure caught up with me and my body began to overheat. I started slowing down again, wondering if I could continue any longer.

Suddenly, I was struck by a sudden wave of ultra-running inspiration. Out of nowhere, a film clip from an old Badwater documentary popped into my head. It was a clip of a runner's crew who sprayed him down with water from a giant machine to keep cool. Although there wasn't a random shed of landscaping equipment that just so happened to sit alongside the course, I did manage to get my hands on a small spray bottle. Who would have thought a spray bottle filled with cold water would have such a positive impact? I sprayed my face and mouth for the rest of the race to prevent myself from overheating.

Things were going well again, and I began finding my groove for the first time in a long time. Yet still, another obstacle arrived. At one point, to cool down, I stuck my head into a cooler filled with ice water. It felt refreshing, but the instant I popped up, blood began pouring from my nose! Nosebleeds became a constant problem for the remainder of the night. I couldn't touch my nose without causing it to bleed, nor could I blow it. Even when gnats flew inside of it, they had to stay there, as it was that or risk another enormous nosebleed.

As I ran with my shirt rolled up and pressed against my nose, I spit misty clouds of blood into the air illuminated by the bright light of my headlamp. Nevertheless, I kept moving forward regardless of the blood, regardless of the blisters, and regardless of the heat. As I like to say: the moment when your legs give up is the exact moment when your heart gives more. From here, it was one foot in front of the other, and one way or another, I crossed the finish line!

My first 200-mile ultramarathon was a race filled with many ups and downs, but no matter what happened, I kept my forward motion *relentless*. When you run 200 miles, the highs can take you to outer space, but the lows can place you in a race-day grave. I knew self-doubt would arise going into the race. However, even when times were tough, I never gave up faith in my abilities to finish. As you can imagine, an ultramarathon can be one big struggle filled with many smaller struggles to overcome.

After the race, when I reached my hotel bed, my legs hurt badly. It was only a few hours until my flight back home and I needed some sleep. So, I went into the hotel room bathroom, laid on the floor, wrapped my upper body in a blanket, and stuck my lower body on the floor of the shower. With a steady flow of ice-cold water falling on my legs, I was able to get a few hours of shut-eye before a painful journey back home.

On the drive over to the airport, as I was enjoying the soothing sound of the rental car air conditioner, I turned on the radio. The broadcaster said, "It's a hot one today, try to stay indoors, and don't do anything physically exerting." This announcement made me smile, providing a small bit of relief to my severely painful and blistered feet.

It took three people asking me about my race in the security line at the airport before I realized the back of my race shirt read "Ask me how far I ran on Labor Day weekend 2018." I was caught off guard by a race full of surprises one last time. Eventually, I made it on the plane, sat down, looked out the window, and smiled. *Yes,* I ran 200 miles! *Yes,* I did so in under seventy-two hours, so *yes,* I did "go all the way."

Running 200 miles is no easy feat; it would be misleading to say it was. However, because of the adversity I faced, I had to dig deep into myself. The will to relentlessly move forward can only come from within. It took a journey through the pitch dark to find the brightest of lights. An illuminated darkness, if you will. It was here where I learned a great lesson. The lesson is this: if you want to move upward, you must first travel downward, and you have to experience this eternal mystery for yourself to fully understand the paradox, that is, the coincidence of opposites. By holding those opposites together, they reconcile and release to relieve your suffering. That's why at times we feel like walking contradictions, because on the level of the mind and body, we are just that. This can create a great deal of pain, stress, and anxiety, negatively affecting our running. This is the beautiful struggle that is ultramarathon running.

Don't worry, *Mindful Ultramarathon Running* will teach you about the art of *letting go* and it will help a great deal. However, you can't just talk about it; to learn how to transcend the pain, you most dive into it, become it, and fall in love with it. Remember, we don't choose to love, we must *let go* and fall into it. We will touch on this concept in a future chapter and I will later reveal the greatest gift of all.

You see, I didn't just run through my body, I ran through my mind, and with my spirit. The pain was unavoidable; however, it took a mindful approach to experience the struggle without falling victim to great suffering. By reading this book, you will soon discover that when running, the pain is inevitable, but suffering is not. Prolonged suffering is a choice.

I've put many of the thoughts, principles, and techniques you are about to read into practice, and the results have extended far beyond my running shoes. That's why I started this book by saying *"I laced up a pair of running shoes to learn how to run; who knew that one day they would teach me how to fly?"* That's what this book will do: give you wings.

You will fly high above your self-limiting thoughts and transcend to running distances far beyond your comprehension. Soon, you will learn to find joy inside your struggles and develop a new mindful-running practice that brings waves of inner peace to your life. Then, maybe when it's all said and done, I will see you on the starting line of your first 100- or 200-mile ultramarathon!

With that, let's take the first step together as you begin a new journey. A journey to increase endurance, run longer, and find inner peace in the process. You may know how the proverb goes:

"A journey of a thousand miles begins with a single step."

—Lao Tzu

CHAPTER 1:

Mindful Ultramarathon Running

Why do you want to run an ultramarathon or even longer distances? What do the miles mean to you? How will your next run work toward transforming your life for the better? Mindful ultramarathon running is a subjective term and carries many different meanings for many different people. Here in this book, and in your new practice, it's about constantly finding answers to the questions you just read. That's because those answers will in turn empower every aspect of your being, which naturally improves how you run. Simply put, mindful ultramarathon running is running ultra distances with thought behind them.

When you run mindfully, you gain a clear understanding that you're in control of your internal environment. You become the observer of thought, instead of the thinker. Now you can eliminate self-limiting beliefs that prevent you from running longer distances. Your thoughts can empower you or enslave you—the choice is yours. As an ultra runner, you already understand this on some level. You know this because if you fell victim to your self-limiting beliefs, well, you'd likely never consider running an ultramarathon. Therefore, you wouldn't be reading these words. Here's another way to explain it: mindful ultramarathon running teaches you how to eliminate limitations on the inside so you can run longer distances on the outside.

Although the idea of mindful ultramarathon running sounds beneficial, you may be asking yourself questions such as "How do I use mindful ultramarathon running practically? Is there a method? Are there any steps to take?" Here's the answer: *yes*. In fact, I'll soon reveal how mindful ultramarathon running can guide you to run extraordinarily long distances. But first, it's crucial to examine the type of questions you are asking yourself on a daily basis. Quality questions will build a solid foundation for your mindful ultramarathon running practice.

Change Your Questions

The better the questions, the better the answers. If you ask a high-level question, you will receive a high-level answer. As you may know, many new runners get caught up in their heads. They ask themselves questions such as "How could someone like me finish a marathon?" or "Why can't I run a mile without stopping?"

These types of self-limiting questions are common for runners. How do I know? Because I've asked similar questions myself. I know they create an intense focus on limitations rather than finding productive ways to achieve your goals. As a result, limited questions continue to stack up, and if you're not careful, the load can become too heavy to handle. Here's where some give up on training. This holds especially true for ultra runners.

Think about it, it's a long way through training, to race day, and across the finish line of an ultramarathon. Yes, you spend a lot of time on your feet, but at the same time, you also spend a lot of time in your mind. That's why it's critical to monitor what's happening in your head. Be the observer, and use your mind as a tool, not an identity. Remember, the physical strength and stamina of your body is an expression of the mental strength and stamina of your mind. For that reason, it's essential to consider the questions you've been asking yourself and whether they encourage progress or leave you idle. Just as a goldfish only grows as big as its tank, you will only run as far as you believe. As I like to say, "first believe that it's possible, and then find the right running shoes for the job."

With that said, let's compare two sample questions below. These examples demonstrate how quality questions can transform your running. Even more so, high-level questions begin to construct the foundation of your new mindful running practice.

Question 1: How can I ever train for a 100-mile ultramarathon as a full-time parent of three?

Question 2: What training program would someone need to be absolutely certain they will have time to train for a 100-mile ultramarathon no matter their schedule?

Do you see the difference? Did you notice how the first question assumes failure while the second expects success? Question number one creates excuses, while question number two encourages solutions. In this example, question number two guides you to find a less time-consuming training program—and who knows, by doing so, you may have stumbled upon another book of mine: *A Runner's Secret*. In that book, I provide a system to run any distance—including 100 miles—by running only one day per week. As you can see, the right answers are available; it just requires asking the right questions.

The fact is, questions trigger a mental reflex. When you ask yourself a question, there's a massive takeover in your brain. When the brain is thinking of a question, it can hardly contemplate anything else until it finds an answer. Here's the point: use better questions to guide you to better results. Soon, your mind becomes the most powerful tool you have for running ultra distances, and you can use it as such, instead of it using you.

Now that you've begun building your mindful ultramarathon running foundation, let's take your practice one step further. Let's discuss the primary objective of mindful ultramarathon running and how to apply it practically.

Find Your Path

Everyone's mindful ultramarathon running journey will be different. You pave your own path. Some will follow what they read here piece by piece to enhance performance, while others will apply it to discover a mental and spiritual connection through the miles. Regardless of how mindful ultramarathon running works for you, there's one constant. That is, sooner or later, as you reach longer ultramarathon distances, your mind and body will merge as one. When this formation occurs, it unlocks the door to your infinite potential, the door to the natural flow of life. That's the door to your spirit, the stillness from within.

When you align with something so infinite, so divine, so majestic, time stops. It's here in the *present moment* where running any distance becomes possible. Even the distance you once thought was impossible. I often like to say, "I never knew I couldn't run a 200-mile ultramarathon, and that's precisely why I was able to run a 200-mile ultramarathon."

To clarify, what you really want to gain from *Mindful Ultramarathon Running* is the knowledge to learn how to run in the NOW. That's because, as I said in the introduction, here, right now, in this moment, measurements such as time and distance do not exist. Can you imagine the advantage this provides in a sport like ultramarathon running? Are you considering the possibilities?

When I took my focus off external achievement and placed it on internal well-being, my entire running experience changed for the better, and so did my life. As you continue reading and enter the stillness of the present moment, you will move more than you ever thought possible.

Running in the Present Moment

To be clear, if there is any kind of goal in mindful ultramarathon running, it's to run in the present moment. A place where every mile is the same mile and you can run extraordinarily long distances. It's how I've run 200 miles straight and seventy-two hours in one race. It's a big reason how I run 50K races with no food or water and how I ran 100 miles in below-freezing temperatures.

In the present moment, running is no longer a build-up-and-release process as it transcends to a journey of love and growth. Moreover, it's my purpose to help you align with your inner self to produce outer results such as finishing a 100- or 200-mile race. You will learn that running isn't as stressful as you may think—and neither is life. I say this because you don't have to face your reality; instead, you can create it. Remember this: it's your choice what to focus on. So, choose to finish, only to finish, and the finish line of any ultra distance will come.

When you run in the present moment and continue to move your feet forward, eventually the finish line comes. This method has never failed once. By running mindfully, sooner or later, that voice telling you to quit loses its dominance. That voice is the *ego*.

To clarify, when I say "ego," I'm *not* referring to the stereotypical description of an individual who holds an inflated sense of self. The ego I'm referring to is any image or story you identify with. Identification usually derives from stories you or others create and you accept as truth. The ego is not bad, as it can provide inner resistance for greater growth. It only becomes problematic when you attach to it.

The key is to observe the ego and use it as a tool. Don't identify with it as "self." This detachment takes focus, but don't worry, running races 100 miles in length will surely give you plenty of practice.

Overcoming the Ego

We expand by demand. Just as pushing heavier weights makes you stronger, you must continue to overcome the ego to tone it down. If not, you will notice that excuses, hesitation, and self-limiting stories come more frequently, and these negative actions are the food of the ego. Think about it, negative actions like complaining, hating, and gossiping create separateness—a falsehood that swerves you away from oneness, from the stillness of the present moment.

The ego, if left unchecked, can persuade you to give up on your ultra running dreams. Think about it, if you never try, then you never have a chance of coming up short—and if you never come up short, then you will never bruise the ego. Yet, by running ultramarathons, it's very possible to face such an enormous amount of suffering that your consciousness has no other choice but to separate from the false self.

As you may come to realize, adversity is a gift and ultra runners know this instinctively.

The Mindful Running Contradiction

The thought of combining mindfulness and ultra running can be confusing. From the outside, mindfulness looks like total relaxation, while running on its own appears stressful and tense. Well, mindfulness allows you to relax while running, and at the same time, become more alert and focused—the result: you are lighter on your feet and faster on your legs. You move with grace and flow through your run. Instead of bouncing back from an empty tank to a full one, your energy dispenses evenly, and you run much longer because of it. To sum it up nicely: behind the calm eyes of every mindful ultramarathon runner lies the focus, clarity, and alertness to run astonishing distances.

By following a mindful running approach, you will learn to overcome negative self-talk. You can step back and look at your thoughts, feelings, and emotions subjectively. Instead of working *against* you, they will now work *for* you in your journey to growing your stamina both physically and mentally. Look, I know, runs come to an end. But you know what? Your journey doesn't. Yes, there are arrivals; however, the journey is infinite. In that sense, so is the potential that lies deep within you.

The path is through the present moment, in which you separate from useless thoughts and distractions. Soon you will remove yourself from both busy and hectic external and internal noises. Now you can train simply for the love of running and finding oneself.

Of course, you'll continuously progress. Growth is in our nature. Progress creates happiness. But rather than fight the current with force, you'll flow downstream with grace. Soon you'll learn to align with the flow, and take it for the ride of your life. Oh, and to the finish line of many ultramarathons to come.

No more judging yourself on distance, speed, or finish lines. No getting hung up on work, emails, and phone calls. No worrying about the hecklers outside your mind . . . and the hecklers inside your mind. Just you and your new vibrant life as a mindful ultramarathon runner. And you know what? When you run with thought behind it, a remarkable shift transpires. As you try *less*, you achieve *more*. What a paradox mindful running can be.

What do I mean, exactly? Well, without knowing it, you eliminate resistance. Not resistance in the form of steeper hills and longer mileage. What I'm referring to is internal resistance. That is, all the stress, negativity, and anxiety that creates dis-ease in your life. By running mindfully, you replace judgment and expectations with love and appreciation. Consequently, from the prolonged mileage of ultra running, you'll become a master of this trade-off.

The change in your running will also extend to your everyday life. It will bring you much more peace, joy, and happiness. Mindful ultramarathon running may be the blessing you've been waiting for all along. It's a humbling journey.

Next, it's time to practice running in the present moment, and it starts before your run, with meditation. In a succeeding chapter, I'll provide instructions for a quick yet powerful prerun meditation to develop momentum and increase energy. For now, the following is a short introduction.

Mindful Running Meditation

Running can be a form of meditation; and in meditation, one learns to stay in the present moment. If you have experience meditating, you may have encountered losing yourself in the moment. It's very possible to fall into a deep trance for hours that only feels like minutes. That's the power of finding the NOW.

Can you imagine how beneficial this shift in your perception of time can be as an ultra runner? I've run one small circle for twenty-four, forty-eight, and seventy-two hours straight, and focusing on the here and now was a big part of that.

As I mentioned, later in this book, I will teach you a powerful prerun meditation that will benefit you in so many ways. The meditation will increase positive energy for longer runs and eliminate internal resistance that blocks usable energy. Most importantly, it will allow you to enter the NOW before your run to transition more easily during it.

Remember, it's not that thoughts of the past and future are a bad thing; it's more about using them as a tool, not a destination. Get in and get out of the past and don't pitch a tent in the future. Neither are your home. When you use the past as a tool, you become humble, and when you live there, you become depressed. When you use the future as a tool, you become motivated, but when you live there, you become anxious. Get the point?

The more you practice meditation, the easier running in the present moment becomes. During meditation, you focus on your breath to detach from your thoughts. And as we learned earlier, clinging on to thoughts during a run will take you into the past and future. As a result, running creates suffering instead of joy.

The Past, Present, and Future

While running, you experience different sensations and urges. These experiences create thoughts, and it's these thoughts that take you out of timelessness, out of oneness. Think about it, if you continuously focus on the finish line, running will feel like an eternity. I can tell you from experience. Whether it's 200, 20, or 2 miles from the finish line, if you get stuck in the future, you suffer.

On the other hand, have you ever done something you really love? Something you are incredibly passionate about? What happens? Hours feel like minutes, do they not? Albert Einstein explains it like this: "Put your hand on a hot stove for a minute, and it seems like an hour. Sit with a pretty girl for an hour, and it seems like a minute." The point is this: in the present moment, time is nonexistent.

I once ran a twelve-hour race with 3 miles of trails per lap. On that day, the last lap felt like the first lap. That's the power of running in the NOW! So, on race day, would you rather run in a dimension where time and distance are unobservable, or obsess over the finish line where every step is a grueling step to the end? I know, it's a leading question, but it provides a definitive answer that makes the point clear.

Sure, you can visit the thought of finishing every so often for motivation. The feeling of crossing the finish line of a new distance is indescribable. I thought crossing the finish line of a 50-mile race was spectacular, that is, until I completed 100 miles. I then thought crossing the finish line of a 100-mile race was the ultimate joy, that is, until I completed 200 miles.

Here's the takeaway: use your mind as a tool to create positive emotions like enthusiasm. Avoid obsessing over the finish line in order to prevent suffering, which can lead to a DNF. Remember, happiness and joy aren't in the future at some proverbial checkpoint we call the finish line. They exist right here, right now, within every stride. When running an ultramarathon, if you find appreciation for the first 99 miles, the hundredth mile comes in no time at all.

As you may know, the present moment is not always easy to stay in. Thoughts, urges, sensations, and emotions are all at play, and if you're not careful, they can pull you out of the present moment while running. To avoid this, head over to the next chapter, where I will teach you a simple process to follow for staying in the present moment.

CHAPTER 2:

Three Steps

When you run and thoughts arise that create suffering, instead of clinging to them, or identifying with the mind, step back and view your thoughts subjectively. Try not to see yourself as the thinker. Instead, be the observer of thought. Older philosophy tells us, "I think, therefore I am," but it's in the NOW where we understand the new-age idea "I am, therefore I think."

As you run, and thoughts arise, follow this three-step mindful running process:

1. Acknowledge the THOUGHT.
2. Don't judge the THOUGHT.
3. Let go of the THOUGHT.

These steps will help you run in the present moment, and the better you get, the longer you will be able run. You can become the creator of your running experience, meaning you will significantly improve at managing the highs and lows on race day.

For example, you can let go of negative thoughts that create negative emotions and enhance positive thoughts that create positive emotions. You will dissolve self-doubt and fear while amplifying joy and enthusiasm. Soon you realize that letting thoughts go through the mind is a mental muscle and the more you train, the easier it becomes.

So what triggers these luring thoughts anyway? They typically stem from sensations, urges, and your senses. Please keep reading to understand each and learn how to let them go in order to avoid prolonged suffering and stay in the present moment. This has the potential to make a training run of a few hours feel like a few minutes.

Sensations on the Run

A sensation is something we feel or perceive physically that makes contact with the body. As you run, you experience many different sensations. Whether it's a slight pain in your foot, the grumbling of your stomach, or the depletion of energy, each sensation can cause thoughts of worry and concern.

For example, you may want to stop training because you develop knee pain. You obsess over the future and convince yourself that this pain will lead to a DNF on race day. Unfortunately, you've just trapped yourself in the future, where quitting your ultramarathon training program becomes a real possibility. That, or it gives you a big enough excuse to give up when things get tough.

However, there's another option. If you observe the sensation in your knee without judgment, you might learn something new. Maybe your stride is too long, which causes you to heel strike, so the longer you run, the greater the amount of pain. Now, instead of giving up, you shorten your stride. As a result, not only does your knee pain disappear, you increase the likelihood of longevity in your running. Never forget these words: ultra runners don't just know how to face the pain; they expect it, and they use the adversity to better themselves.

By clinging to every sensation, you'll get nowhere fast. Extreme distances deliver extreme stress. The excessive mileage creates everything from pain in your feet to weird feelings in your stomach. However, most of these sensations go away when you direct your attention elsewhere. When sensations occur that create disempowering thoughts, follow the same mindful running process to stay in the present moment:

1. Acknowledge the SENSATION.

2. Don't judge the SENSATION.
3. Let go of the SENSATION.

I try not to overthink the causes of sensations while running. Instead, I acknowledge each sensation without making assumptions. Whether it's an itch on my leg, stabbing pain in my side, or a tingling feeling in my hands, I let it go, slow down, and continue moving forward. Yes, the sensation could be a real problem, but it could also be nothing at all.

Senses on the Run

Next, while running ultra distances, you'll experience the world through your five senses: touch, sight, sound, smell, and taste. Whether it's the sound of your feet, the sight of a tree, the smell of morning air, the feeling of wind, or the taste of a drink, practice noticing them; by doing so, you will anchor into the present moment.

Your body and its senses are how you experience your run. Here's the key: see them for what they are but not more than what they are. Meaning, name them "touch," "sight," "sound," "smell," and "taste." Notice each sense and if disempowering thoughts begin to arise from any of them, follow the same process for staying in the present moment:

1. Acknowledge the SENSE.
2. Don't judge the SENSE.
3. Let go of the SENSE.

Think about it, the organs associated with each sense delivers information to the brain, and every piece of information can be interpreted or perceived differently. Use the process when needed and continue running forward.

Urges on the Run

This is a big one for ultra runners. You will face many urges that prevent you from finishing your run. As urges develop, you have to cope with the temptations and let them pass. You will have urges to stop, quit, and throw in the towel. Urges to speed up when you should slow down and slow down when you should speed up.

31

You may have addictive behaviors in the kitchen, such as eating yourself into a sugar coma. Similarly, you might find comfort at an aid station instead of dealing with the uncomfortable while running. It's likely you'll face the urge to hit the snooze button and quit your training schedule at some point. Any poor lifestyle habits can prevent you from progressing. Again, when these urges occur, in any form, follow the same process to stay in the present moment:

1. Acknowledge the URGE.
2. Don't judge the URGE.
3. Let go of the URGE.

Notice how your body feels when facing an urge; for example, wanting to stop at the 100K during a 100-mile race or desiring to sit in your warm car during a below-freezing winter twenty-four-hour race. When you're freezing, exhausted, and sleep-deprived, you'll want to give up and go home where it's warm and stress-free. But remember, the pain from a DNF is much greater than any stress you face on race day.

Instead of wishing the urge away, develop absolute certainty it will pass. Because guess what? It will! It always does. Cope with the craving and set it free. When something is more powerful than our will to deny it, we are addicted. By following the three-step mindful ultra-running process, you can become an addiction-free runner.

Measure through Emotions

If we know anything as ultra runners, it's the highs and lows of life. During an ultramarathon, one minute you might feel incredible, like you're a superhuman defying the laws of the universe, and the next you might feel down in the dumps, wondering why on earth you would ever put yourself through such a tortuous experience.

On race day, you can feel joy, frustration, enthusiasm, and anger, as well as excitement, hopelessness, happiness, and fear. But regardless of the emotions you feel, know they are a physical reflection of your thoughts and use them as a guide to what you're thinking.

If you feel hopelessness while racing, it's very possible you are identifying with some seriously negative thoughts. Yet the same time, even with emotions, you must accept them without judgment, and let them pass to stay in the present moment. When you face negative emotions, follow the same process to stay in the present moment:

1. Acknowledge the EMOTION
2. Don't judge the EMOTION.
3. Let go of the EMOTION.

Emotions are energy in motion. They are the physical reflection of the thoughts in your mind. When you begin to gain experience with letting go of emotions, you gain control of them, thus gaining control of your energy. Eventually, you learn how to use thoughts and emotions to your advantage while running ultra distances. You ride the positive emotions like a wave and flip the negative ones to positive. It's like taking a natural performance supplement, but the energy doesn't come in powder form. It comes from your heart.

By running in the present moment, you learn to turn your emotions on and off like a light switch. Instead of being a product of your circumstance, you create it. You become the producer of your running experience, you craft your destiny, you create the narrative of your life. Like the best fiction books of all time, your story takes place in two worlds, and as an ultra runner, those worlds are the "be" and the "could be." Please don't ever let it be the "could not."

Let Go and Flow

Overall, you will discover which emotions, thoughts, and feelings create joy (running in the present moment; creating higher levels of energy), and which ones create suffering (living in the past and future; identifying with the mind).

You now have the process, but try not to force it. Yes, pay attention and work through the three steps. However, you should also understand that the act of surrender is required to master the art of letting go. It's more graceful than forceful. You *allow* rather than *accomplish*. In other words, try not to see it as something you do, but instead as something you align with. Become one with your being. Remember, you are a human *being*, not a human *doing*.

Will you become a master overnight? Of course not. You will need to overcome many internal barriers. A limitation is not a wall to break down, it's a gate to let down. Don't smash through a barrier to run longer, instead, *let go of your grip.*

Emotions come and go, and so do the thoughts that create them. However, instead of identifying yourself with your mind—thoughts, emotions, and unconscious, compulsive cycles—you can eventually observe the mind from the stillness, and it's here where you find the present moment.

Remember, the longer you can stay in the NOW, the easier it becomes. So keep at it. If you take a step back for a few runs or miss a few meditations, just pick up where you left off. It's a journey to travel, so make your way back to the path. Sometimes your mind needs a break, like how your legs need to recover. It's not about perfection, it's about progress. Run far and enjoy the journey along the way!

As I often say: one day I let go and forward I ran.

CHAPTER 3:

Self-Discovery

Up until this very moment, you may have been following a very different path as an ultramarathon runner. A way that leads to physical obstacles like burnout, injury, and nausea, and at the same time, mental resistance like boredom, unfulfillment, and tremendous self-doubt. As you now know, this is not the path of a mindful ultramarathon runner.

Regardless of the negativity you face, it's time to resurrect the inner runner buried deep within. The one who's scratching at the surface. The one that you hold back, in fear of becoming too vulnerable, too accepting, too free.

When you begin to let go of old self-limiting beliefs, while aligning with your true self, deep down, it brings you for the ride of a lifetime. You connect with that infinite energy source, that spirit, that love, that natural flow of life. When this occurs, you'll take a leap of faith into the 100 and 200-mile distance without hesitation. You do so because your performance is no longer based on how bad you want it. Now, it's on how much inner resistance you eliminate to make room for more positive energy.

For that reason, one day, you become an experienced runner who made extraordinary progress and it hits you. You realize every one of your goals was not reached by crossing one finish line at a time, but by overcoming one struggle at a time. What a humbling experience running can be, and it all starts with your new path.

Time to Run Farther

How do some ultra runners cover such extraordinary distances over and over again? Why do some runners not only run 100-mile races, but repeat their triumph countless times? What are they doing differently? What is the secret path to developing the relentless forward motion to follow through on your running goals every time, all the time?

Here's the answer: *the path to self-discovery*. That is, running to find out who you really are. This is a paradigm shift for many. It's not that you are actually creating a new you; instead, you're aligning with the real you; your higher self; your inner runner. Because under the fear and conditioning of the mind lies the observer, and it's the observer who uses the body as a vehicle and the mind as a tool to reach extraordinarily long distances.

When running deep into a 200-mile race, there are times I feel a complete separation from the body and mind, in addition to an intense connection with the infinite sky. I'm the consciousness propelling myself into action. The body is the vehicle, the mind is the steering, and my awareness is the GPS. When this takes place, I've connected with the natural flow of life, and I can now float through the miles for days.

From running over one hundred ultra distances, I've observed three stages on my path to self-discovery through ultra running. By becoming consciously aware of each stage, I tapped into what felt like an everlasting source of motivation to follow through on training and races. But first, know the ultramarathon community is quickly expanding. The fact is a growing number of runners are headed in that direction. People are looking for more satisfaction in their lives, and it seems that ultramarathon running has been filling that void.

Whether it's the social isolation, an increase of self-esteem, or the struggle that creates growth, in ultra running, self-discovery might not just be a possibility; for most, it may be the sole purpose of taking on such a challenge in the first place. And here's the good news: becoming an ultra runner who runs distances of 100 miles or longer can happen quicker than you may think.

One day you're running a few miles down the street while looking at the same old cracks in the road. You glance over at the same bushes along your neighborhood pavement and gaze at the same big yellow house on the corner. Then suddenly . . . you are hit with a wave of desire. The desire to *run farther,* and so it begins.

The Universal Principle of Ultra Running

Different runners use different techniques to run ultra distances. However, they all understand one universal principle. They know the magic of holding on just a little longer. Running until you can't take another step, and then taking one more: that's the essence of ultramarathon running. Except it goes far beyond one more step. When running an ultramarathon, you must run as far as you possibly can and then run 50 more miles. The mileage is arbitrary, but the point is valid.

I'll never forget my first official ultramarathon race. It was 50 miles in length. It's shocking when you first learn the difference between an ultramarathon and a regular marathon. During your first marathon, you likely reach somewhere around mile 16 and think "how on earth am I going to finish this race?" At the time, the remaining 10 miles seems astronomical. That is, until you enter the world of ultramarathon running.

When you run a 50-mile ultramarathon, the same doubt creeps in around mile 24. You think to yourself, "Wow, I thought a marathon was tough. I'm exhausted and I still have almost an entire marathon to go!" This same realization scales to longer distances like your first 100K and 100 miles as well.

The point is that for ultramarathon runners, pushing the limits is what we are designed to do. We don't know any other way. It's in every ounce of our being. As you become more enduring, your perspective of time and distance transforms. One day you might be driving down the highway with 100 miles remaining in your trip, when you think, "are we there yet?" Then eventually your thought becomes "I could run that."

Running an ultramarathon mindfully will not only change your perspective on these relative forms of measurement, it will begin to change your perspective on who you are. The great suffering you experience disrupts your thought patterns and catapults your consciousness from your false self. If you are not your false self, then who are you? Ultra running is undoubtedly one way to find out.

The Path to Self-Discovery

Ultra running creates an intense struggle to find a deeper meaning of self. It's similar to the many ancient stories of a person leaving home, going through an enormous struggle, and returning with a deeper understanding of life, and most importantly, a deeper understanding of who they are. The characters in these stories eventually realize what they have been searching for has been inside them all along.

Self-discovery is not only what propels us as ultramarathon runners, it's a motivation for everyday life. At least, it is for those who step outside the mind and become consciously aware of their thoughts.

Going deep into oneself will help you run longer and see your planned distance all the way through. You'll take those extra steps and run those extra miles until eventually all your efforts begin to create a path. That path leads to a discovery, a discovery of self, and you may be fortunate enough to find that person you've been running toward all along.

It is called self-discovery, and it's a natural path you'll find in ultra running as you continue to run longer distances. It has the potential to provide abundance of meaning and drive if you let it. That's because we can only be motivated by what sits on the surface for so long. Achievement, pride, and significance are just a few of the examples. So we keep digging, moving our feet forward, traveling higher, lower, and longer. We continue our search farther and beyond.

The search alone has the potential to take you to extraordinary distances. My personal journey guided me to run 200 miles multiple times. It was a distance of unfathomable depths that was both humbling and hellacious, gratifying and grueling, rewarding and rigorous.

In the process of running ultra distances, you learn a lot about what drives you. But most importantly, you learn to look inward for motivation, not outward. I say this because outward motivation only lasts for so long. But if you find something to hold on to deep within, you develop inspiration, in spirit. The word *inspiration* comes from the Latin world *inspirare* meaning "divine guidance." In this way, motivation is brief, inspiration is forever. You can run distances you once couldn't comprehend, let alone take a shot at trying.

It's absolutely essential to focus on getting to know who you are in the process and being comfortable with that person. Living as the real you makes reaching a new distance less like a quantum leap and more like a hopscotch jump. This holds true for jumping from 50K to 50 miles, 50 miles to 100 miles, and 100 miles to 200 miles. As you can see, in ultra running, you do not progress elegantly to your next distance, you double it!

It takes faith in the unknown to run a new ultramarathon distance, and most importantly, it takes faith in yourself to do so. Standing at the 200-mile starting line, I didn't have a clue if I could cover such an extraordinary distance. I had no idea at all. However, what I did have was faith. I had faith in myself and faith in the unknown.

Although training only lasted for so long, looking back, it now feels like I was training for a 200-mile race for as far back as I can remember and I never knew it. It was just one more arrival down the path of discovering who I was as a runner and finding out who I was as a human being. Most people don't know when they are on the road to self-discovery. All you have is an intuitive compass to get you there. Ultra running strips you down bare, past the PRs, race shirts, and finisher medals. Struggle, growth, pain, and pleasure—it's the human experience in its rawest form.

Ultra running is a continuous journey from one distance to another. It provides you with new building blocks to construct yourself into a runner who is certain of one thing. You become sure that running *any* distance is possible for *anyone* if they want it bad enough. So please allow me to ask you one simple question. The question is this: How bad do you want it?

On your path to self-discovery you'll soon realize that as you trek down those trails and crank out those miles, you enter into a dilemma. It seems the closer you get to finding yourself, the further away you get. Or better put, you must *lose yourself* before you can *find yourself.*

Tick-Tock on the Self-Discovery Clock

You must *lose* yourself before you can *find* yourself. I know, it sounds a bit paradoxical, sort of like a controlled accident, but hear me out. Most don't live as themselves, they live the way they think others think they should live. It's like we leave the twelve o'clock hour on the clock of life as ourselves and as we age we move further and further away from who we really are. Using the clock example, six o'clock would be the furthest from self as possible.

We try new things and meet new people, but in the process, we unconsciously take on a *role* we think we should play to please others, to avoid rejection, or to be loved. Unknowingly, we become a copy of our parents, friends, or society's beliefs. As a result, our thoughts are no longer our own. We literally live as someone who we *think* we should be or who we *think* someone else *thinks* we should be rather than the someone we truly are. All the while we unconsciously search for a way back to our true selves. We look for a way back home, a way back to twelve o'clock.

It's like an unconscious game of hide-and-seek. We believe the path to fulfillment will create a path to self-discovery, but for most, we are too deep in the woods of our unconscious routines to find a way out. We spend years on a metaphorical manhunt navigating through the maze with a blindfold on. We live a lukewarm life looking for the fire that feeds our most burning desires. The light that feeds our souls. But here's the trap: *there is no path.*

Wait, what? No path? How could there be no path to self-discovery? Well, there isn't a path *yet.* Following a prepaved path will lead you nowhere fast. If there is a path to follow, then it's someone else's path.

You must find your own path, no matter how difficult the road less traveled becomes. *Your* path is *your* path and all the good and bad that comes with it.

Everyone wants to see the view from the top of the mountain, but all the happiness and growth occurs when you're climbing it. Sooner or later, each step we take toward our passion fuels us further, as progress is one of the main ingredients to happiness. The closer you come to fulfillment, the more you fill the empty hole toward becoming your whole self, and the closer you tick back toward twelve o'clock.

Yes, progress is a large contribution to happiness, and isn't that the secret to an exceptional life? A life of progress toward fulfillment? If you ever want to feel like a superhuman ultra runner, then strive to become one of meaning, purpose, and fulfillment. As I like to say, we all have a gift to contribute to the world, and when you recognize your gift, a purpose is born. Simply put, there are not many forces more powerful than an ultra runner fueled by a great purpose.

That's why you've been promised the pursuit of happiness and not happiness itself. That's because happiness is actually in the pursuit; it's in progress, it's in growth. There's no pot of gold at the end of the rainbow, just a beautiful incline to climb and grow from.

Now, back the clock example; there are two distinct factors to consider as your clock keeps ticking:

1. Eventually, you *wake up*. The hour hand keeps ticking and you head back to your true self, back to twelve o'clock. You find the path to fulfillment and every step becomes a progressive step toward self-discovery. Or should I say your *rediscovery*?

Or . . .

2. You get lost in the hour hands of life, and your clock stops ticking before making it back to twelve o'clock. Even if you consider your life a success. If you reach the end of a successful life but are entirely unfulfilled, then you have discovered true disappointment and regret.

Carl Jung, a famous Swiss psychiatrist and psychoanalyst who founded analytical psychology, explains it brilliantly by stating, "The first half of life is devoted to forming a healthy ego, the second half is going inward and letting go of it."

Fortunately, that's where mindful ultramarathon running can play a crucial role in self-discovery. You run from the inside out rather than the outside in. In this way, the long mileage teaches you firsthand how to deal with suffering in a productive way to speed up your clock and keep it moving forward. That's because ultra runners do not just reach outside their comfort zone, they live there. We live outside the realm of the possible searching for our next impossible feat, and though the stresses of struggle and pain you begin to wake up.

Ultra Running Will Wake You Up

Ultra running has the potential to wake you up to who you really are by allowing you to let go of who you imagine yourself to be. An "awakening" if you will. As a result, you develop into a person who can recognize limiting beliefs. You understand that if you are the one who created them, then you are the one who can change them.

Isolation can be a wonderful thing. With the time spent alone through the struggle, discomfort, and pain, you learn more about yourself than anyone could ever tell you, and you can learn more about life through a 100-mile race than any book could ever teach you.

Ultra running then becomes a purification process if you let it. You'll grow more sensitive to resistance in all forms. You can literally feel anything that tries to stop you from continuing on the road to that 50-, 100-, or 200-mile finish line. No longer are you only conscious of how physical resistance expends energy, but you'll also notice the draining effects of mental resistance as well.

Resistance in all forms requires energy, this holds especially true during the later stages of a race. Toward the end of an ultramarathon, you'll feel the resistance, whether physical, mental, or spiritual. Even your thoughts can create stressful emotions that use up energy.

Think about it, emotions are created by thoughts. Feelings like fear, sadness, and happiness all come from the thoughts you think. Have you ever considered what the word emotion means? The word *emotion* comes from the Latin word *movere* meaning "move" or "in motion." Emotions are literally your thoughts in motion. Motion in all forms requires energy . . . and yes, that includes your feelings.

So how does this relate to purification? Well, the longer you run the more sensitive you become to resistance. You naturally start to eliminate that which does not serve you and endure that which does. Now you run farther distances with what feels like less effort because, in a sense, it takes less work. In other words, you've let go of the baggage. You'll now feel lighter on your feet and less tense in the face.

Eventually, you clearly see the negative impact of different resistances in your life. From bad relationships, to resentment toward others, to harmful compulsions or even eating processed foods. You can't help but see the problematic habits and addictions you've developed. You see them because you feel them, and you naturally raise your vibrations any way you can.

This could even mean giving up someone in your life who is close to you. Suddenly, you wake up to the negative impact they have on you and see the relationship is doing more harm than good. Have you ever worked around negative people? They consume more of your energy than just about any other kind of resistance on the planet. Some people are energy consumers and will absorb it any chance they get. Remember, there are two ways to create a higher building. You can work at building it taller, or you can knock down the other buildings around you. Never forget this.

Although, in mindful ultramarathon running, we also see resistance as a way to grow. You naturally adopt a growth mindset. Even those challenging people can help shape you into the person you want to become. Just like weights in a gym, resistance like stress, adversity, and problems are a part of life to help you grow. You can either eliminate the resistance or use it for growth, but dwelling and stressing about it will only absorb more energy. The energy that's required to live a healthy and happy life—and to run ultramarathon distances.

All types of resistance are endured, survived, and coped with by the ultra runner. You must deal with it, or let it linger in the mind, causing it to magnify greatly during the real long distances. This ultimately creates a harder race than the race was intended to be. Even the mildest of adversity will escalate massively if not controlled.

We as ultra runners don't just struggle though the miles. We struggle through the physical and mental roller coasters of adversity on our path to receiving a more revealing and absolute understanding of our inner and most intimate selves. When we are led by self-discovery, we develop a mindset where ultramarathon running is not only what you do, it's a part of who you are. This transformation occurs through three stages.

Three Stages to Discovery

As you run the path to self-discovery and monitor it mindfully, you'll notice there are three stages: *run to prove to others*, *run to prove to yourself*, and finally, *run to find yourself.* Which stage are you on? Keep reading to find out.

Stage 1: Run to Prove to Others

Early on in our running, we tend to run so we can prove ourselves to others. This can be highly effective when you first start off, and yes, you can reach farther distances by using it. Yet over the long run it's a *trap*, and if you are not careful, you could spend an eternity there.

Fortunately, most people will break free of this by pushing themselves to greater depths. But to be safe, how does one assure their escape? Simple: stop holding someone else's opinion of you higher than your own. It's easy to say you don't, but the truth is . . . most do. Whether it be your friends, family, coworkers, or even total strangers . . . most of us care greatly about other people's opinions.

Here's the problem: proving yourself to others feels like a never-ending process. There are billions of people on this planet and the fact is not everyone is going to like you or find your running impressive. As a result, running to prove yourself to others will wear you out. It creates stress in your running, making it more of an acidic process then one of health and wellness. Too much of it can be corrosive.

Also, as you search for inspiration through many different outlets, be careful as to what you feed your mind. Stand guard at the entrance of your mind. Sayings like "prove them wrong" may be a short-term motivator, and it sure fuels you in the "prove to others" stage. Sure, you can run longer distances with this type of mentality, but for how long? How long will it last?

I'm sure even some of the best endurance runners use this motivator at times. I'm not sure if it ever goes away 100 percent. Yet, if this is what primarily drives you, then achieving longevity in your ultra running career will be damaging. It can bring more harm to your life than good.

Depending on where your experiences, this may or may not resonate with you. Some runners will even become comfortable and choose to stay here. However, if you keep running farther, especially toward the 100-mile distance and beyond, the desire to prove yourself to others will significantly reduce.

As I mentioned, there will be times you'll run to prove yourself to others, and it can be useful if controlled and limited. Even so, eventually, it can't continue as your primary motive. Remember, if you are looking for longevity in your running, and want to run extraordinarily long distances, finding a purer purpose will make the impossible much more possible.

Sooner or later, you may see the seeking of approval from others for the addiction it is and feel exhausted because of it. It consumes a substantial amount of energy. You will see the unneeded resistance it creates in your training, and likely begin looking for something more profound that drives you.

Don't forget, the trap is when you value someone else's opinion of yourself more than you value your own. Soon, if you keep focus on running mindfully, on your path to self-discovery, at some point, there's a realization that you are not living as you, and you will wake up. From here, running will evolve from proving yourself to others, to proving yourself to you. So, you keep on running.

Stage 2: Run to Prove to Yourself

Running to prove something to yourself can be remarkably influencing. As you continue directing your energy inward, naturally, you will feel more energized. Pretty simple right? Focusing on *other people* while running gives your energy to *other* people; focusing on *yourself* while running gives your energy to *yourself.* You start developing an enormous amount of energy to run even longer ultra distances than you may have already.

There's an old saying: "energy flows where attention goes." By shifting your focus away from others and back to yourself, you stop wasting your energy on the opinions of others. You stop working toward some imaginary attaboy and begin focusing on what *you* feel and what *you* think of yourself. It's here where you begin developing an elite mindset.

When you start listening to your body, you begin changing the way you run. You make quicker and more effective decisions in your running when you are tuned into your body. You start taking action on *intuition,* and this might be the greatest secret of all. Following your intuition and listening to your body will improve your running drastically. It can take you farther than any supplement or piece of advice ever could. You'll run longer distances on *your* terms, and you will enjoy doing so. Running for the joy of running is quite transcending.

As I mentioned earlier, I've run over one hundred ultra distances within a handful of years. How did I do it? The answer: by loving the process while enjoying the journey. Most importantly, I did it by being *grateful* for life.

Consider this: you're living on a flying blue rock that rotates around a gigantic ball of fire. It's said that the odds of being born as "you" are 1 in 400 trillion! You hit the intergalactic lottery; life is a *miracle,* be grateful for that alone!

Running to prove something to yourself not only provides more energy, it creates a more proficient runner, capable of running incredible distances. But where does it stop? How much do you need to prove until you are satisfied? Is there an end? You're not sure so you keep running. You race at ultramarathon distances. You train at ultramarathon distances. You crank out long run after long run. Running strips you down more and more until one day you think, "Why do I need to prove anything to myself, and wait, who am I anyway?"

You realize you haven't been you at all, only what you *imagine* yourself to be. Playing a "character" in the book of life and the person you've been trying to convince is just an illusion of the mind. As you start becoming more consciously aware of being conscious, things start expanding and the boundaries between the possible and the impossible dissolve.

You feel lost, so you start running to find yourself, and here's when things start really falling into place. Here is where true running longevity is found. Here is where running distances like 200 miles become not just a possibility, but your reality. Remember, the inner limits of your mind are the outer limits of your reality. If you can observe your thoughts, then you can reshape your life and suddenly running ultramarathon distances becomes a common practice, and so, you keep on running.

Stage 3: Run to Find Yourself

"Will running help me find myself?"

Maybe you've asked yourself a question like this. Or perhaps it's just a feeling of emptiness you seek to fill. Fortunately, you're already making progress because you now know the answer comes from within. So you run farther and layers of who you imagine yourself to be begin to come off one at a time. You get closer and closer to your true self. Then you run farther, and another layer comes off, and so on, until one day you run that 100- or 200-mile distance and realize something. You realize energy is everlasting.

That's because past the atoms and subatomic particles is energy—*pure energy*, and that same energy that's within me is the same energy that's within you. And that same energy that's in you is the same energy that's in the trees along the trails and in the birds in the sky.

When you become consciously aware of this universal energy field, you no longer run from self, but from *all.* That is, from oneness. You can feel the energy through a universal connection, and now you don't just have the energy within you. You come to realize *you are energy,* and you can now run *any* distance, even 200 miles and longer! It's never been a matter of finding more energy to do it; it's been a matter of understanding you are the energy to do it. Now go run and tell me how you feel! Because when energy is the very essence of your being, how could you ever lose it?

Soon you master the art of running in the present moment. This is one of the greatest secrets of superendurance athletes. You forget about pace, let go, and allow grace to fill your space. As you wake up, you begin to see everything *around* you is the same as what is *within* you. Therefore, when you strip down through the pain and struggle, while pushing yourself to the limits where it literally feels as if you're looking death square in the eyes, do you know what happens? Do you know what you desire most?

The answer is *a simple life.*

Yes, you desire just what a human *being* is here to do: *be.* That's it. You desire to be a good friend, to marry the love of your life, to look your newborn child in the eyes for the first time, to do something kind for a stranger. You desire to shed a tear of sadness, to love until it hurts, to care enough to get angry, and to laugh the night away.

Then you realize maybe . . . just maybe you're not here to *find* yourself at all . . . but maybe . . . just maybe, you are here, as a human *being* to *be* yourself. That's it. To be an extension of something infinitely larger than you. Running ultramarathon distances becomes a reminder of just that: to live a simple life designed by that shared energy that's within us all. Like the popular spiritual statement goes: *We are not human beings having a spiritual experience. We are spiritual beings having a human experience.*

The real secret to self-discovery is that shared energy, and that energy is spirit . . . that energy is *love*. The realization of oneness, this is love. Yes, *love* is the secret to running extraordinary distances and to living an extraordinary life. Love for others, love for your passions, but most importantly . . . love for yourself.

When you love yourself, you become comfortable being yourself with all your quirks and perceived "weaknesses" because that's what makes you who you are, and that's what guides you to your *gift* to the world. That gift is *you*. Now you have found your purpose in life and feel fulfilled as you fall in love with the simplicity of life. And what could be simpler than putting one foot in front of the other? That's the beauty of mindful ultramarathon running. Wouldn't you agree?

Circle Back Home

After we reach the final stage and discover who we really are, beyond the words on this page, I mean *really* experience and *really* feel it, we then circle back to living life, loving, and doing the simple things like running.

Now you're running back down the street looking at the same old cracks in the road. You glance over at the same bushes along your neighborhood pavement and gaze at the same big yellow house on the corner, and again, you are hit by a sudden wave. But this time not of desire, but of *presence*, a wave of *being*. Pure and unintentional presence, and that's the most magnificent fulfillment life could ever offer—and now, you can run for a lifetime.

"Everything is energy, and that's all there is to it. Match the frequency of the reality you want, and you cannot help but get that reality. It can be no other way. This is not philosophy. This is physics"

—Albert Einstein

I leave off here, eager to love and run, with these final words of the chapter:

When you are out running those endless miles, and gazing up into the endless sky, if you fall in love with the endless journey, then your endurance will have no end.

CHAPTER 4:

Mental Mapping

T *he eternal bliss of the 100-mile ultramarathon has a hold of my heart. Running into the sunrise is a marvelous sight. After a half day of chasing my shadow, the sun begins to set, and I'm still running. Into the darkness I go, it's an adventurous journey.*

While it's time to sleep, my feet are awake, relentlessly moving forward. My legs scream to stop. Even so, my eyes remain fixated at the moon as I contemplate our place in the stars.

Eventually, the morning approaches. You can't see the sun, but you feel its presence. The warmth of a new day rushes the course, and you gain a new appreciation for life. The sun then peeks out from a distant cloud as it radiates so profoundly that you can't help but feel the rebirth of a new day. And then it happens. You experience a transformation, a self-transcendent experience. You ran for an entire day straight! What a journey.

As the passage above demonstrates, running a 100-mile ultramarathon is transformational. Race day is an exceedingly painful yet uniquely gratifying experience like no other. The distance can drain you both physically and mentally. Some will give up, and others will persist to the end. But what makes the difference? How do you stay in the race long enough to reach the finish line? How do you find that transcendent experience? How do you avoid a DNF?

Well, although it takes an extraordinary enduring body to run 100 miles or longer, it also takes an extraordinary enduring mind. Think about it, the body doesn't have the last say before giving up. The body doesn't go limp on the course of an ultramarathon; however, the mind sure can. It's your mind that makes the decision to quit and walk back to the car. Remember, the mind is the most powerful tool you have. The same way you focus on moving forward physically, you also do so mentally.

In fact, after running several 100-mile races and longer, I've come up with something I'd like to call "mental mapping." Actually, this frame of mind can be used for any new distance. Whether you're running your first 50K on the pavement, or a 100-mile mountain race in the sky. Simply put, you learn how to run an ultramarathon with your mind, and use it to reach even farther ultramarathon distances. Read on for your new mental mapping system.

Mental Mapping

I'm sure we can all agree that when fixated on the finish line, running an ultramarathon can feel like an eternity. As you can imagine, this leaves your mind vulnerable to wandering. A wandering mind can be a dangerous mind on race day, yet with a little direction, it can be the most powerful tool you have. If you don't focus your thoughts strategically, the voice telling you to stop will shout louder and louder.

When running any kind of race, there's a clear physical path: the beginning, middle, and end. There's course markings, volunteers, and maps. Most race organizations provide plenty of tools to steer you from start to finish. The physical guidance is hand-delivered. With that, you will have the physical side of an ultramarathon covered. But what about the mental side? How do you prevent your mind from running circles instead of forward like your body? How do you stop yourself from choosing that persuasive DNF? How do you decide to leave an aid station while suffering from extreme exhaustion? The answer: you can use a mental map.

This map doesn't come with admission. It's a course you must create within the boundaries of your mind, and I will happily be your guide. This mental approach will significantly reduce your chance of a DNF and provide a remarkable type of energy on race day. Remember, your body doesn't give up on race day; it's your mind that has the final say. Here's what I can tell you from experience: the majority of any run is done from within, not without. In other words, the right mindset can overcome any physical adversities you face in training and on race day. That holds true even when you slip into the lowest of lows.

I've faced extreme nausea, intense cramping, torturous chafing, excessive nosebleeds, unbearable blisters, painful injuries, sleep deprivation, heat exhaustion, and many other race day obstacles. And although you must make physical adjustments on the fly, it's the mind that runs through the pain without losing faith that inside every struggle lies the path to significant growth. It was the philosopher Seneca who said, "Difficulties strengthen the mind, as labor does the body." I've had plenty of opportunities to give up physically; however, I've also placed a tremendous emphasis on emotional intelligence. I've always found the strength from within and used my mind consciously to overcome even the worst-case scenarios.

During each race, I do my best to reach a positive emotional state and ride it like a wave. A positive thought is one thousand times more powerful than a negative one. I say this because a positive thought reflects the principle of creation, while a negative thought reflects the principle of destruction. You see, although I generate positive emotions to empower my running, I never could express it fully in words. I could never adequately describe what type of energy I was tapping into. This same internal energy helped me continue running on mile 150 of a 200-mile race with blisters the size of water balloons on my feet.

Then one day I found myself reading a very profound book titled *The Power of Now* by Eckhart Tolle. I picked up a copy before my first 200-mile ultramarathon. Considering the long length of the race, I was looking for some advice for staying in the present moment. I consider a book like this one to be in the category of "self-transcendence." The *Oxford English Dictionary* defines *self-transcendence* as "the overcoming of the limits of the individual self and its desires in spiritual contemplation and realization." If self-transcendence is a new concept to you, I suggest reading up on the Self-Transcendence 3100 Mile Race. It's the longest certified footrace in the world, created by the late Sri Chinmoy.

Anyway, intrigued by the mystery of suffering and joy, eventually, I read more about three states: *enthusiasm, enjoyment*, and *acceptance*. Eckhart tells us, *"if you are not in the state of either acceptance, enjoyment, or enthusiasm, look closely and you will find you are creating suffering for yourself and others."*

I then had a realization. When running with the mind, you can tap into these three states of being for internal energy on race day. Aligning with one of these three states will allow you to avoid intense struggling. Or at the very least, they are useful tools to pull yourself out of a low on race day. For example, during a 100-mile ultramarathon, you start the race with enthusiasm. Eventually, you fall into enjoyment, and at your lowest, you accept your circumstances until you find your way out. Anything less than acceptance and you're in the danger zone.

So, your "mental map" is guiding your mind back and forth between *enthusiasm, enjoyment*, and *acceptance* during an ultramarathon. If you've ever said "Running makes me feel alive!" then guess what? You're about to find out why. I now see the many times I broke free of unbearable mental suffering during an ultramarathon by tapping into either enthusiasm, enjoyment, or acceptance. So continue reading and learn how to put your mental map in place during your next ultramarathon in order to move from start to finish while avoiding a DNF.

Applying Mental Mapping

The three states of being for your next ultramarathon are *enthusiasm, enjoyment*, and *acceptance*. This is your mental map. Tap into one of the three and your mind will guide your body to the finish line. Let's dig deeper into each stop on your mental map so you have a better understanding of how to apply this method on race day.

State #1: Enthusiasm

When you run with enthusiasm, you feel like a projected dart propelling with enormous intensity straight to its target. In other words, running an ultramarathon with enthusiasm provides enormous energy toward the finish line. When you run with enthusiasm, the concept of winning and losing vanishes. Enthusiasm isn't based on exclusion, it's based on inclusion, and that goes for the obstacles you face on race day as well.

What do I mean exactly? Well, at some point during an ultramarathon, especially at the 100-mile distance or longer, the day becomes more about solving problems than clocking miles. Issues with nutrition, gear, and other race-ending variables eventually arise. Yet, with enthusiasm, you never encounter an unsolvable problem; you always see a way around it. Excuses that might otherwise persuade you to stop running slip out of your psyche as you see them for what they really are: excuses.

Enthusiasm turns energy-draining running into energy-producing running. Most of the time, we start the race with enthusiasm, which can develop from running a new distance or a bucket-list race, or attempting a personal best. Whatever the reason, there's no shortage of enthusiasm at the starting line of an ultramarathon. Although your enthusiasm can last awhile, you will most likely outrun it. Distances like 100 miles are unusually long, so it's rather difficult to remain enthusiastic the entire time. To help you stay enthusiastic for longer periods, let's break it down for ultra running.

The Meaning of Enthusiasm

When you have enthusiasm for ultra running, you have a great vision for how to transform into the runner you know you can be. Remember this: when you find enjoyment in your race and work toward reaching the finish line, you tap into the power of enthusiasm. On the other hand, if you run toward the finish line with no enjoyment, then you create added suffering for yourself.

Consider goals you've set that weren't enjoyable. Maybe you decided to earn a degree in a field you had little interest in. Let's say it was a business degree. Although you don't enjoy business, you pushed yourself through classes anyway. You didn't love accounting, yet you dragged yourself to class every Tuesday night. In this sense, school became a stressful environment.

Next, think of a topic you loved learning about with a goal in mind. Maybe it was a healthy cooking class. Perhaps you loved to cook and had an incredible vision to live a healthier life. As you can imagine, when you enjoy the subject and are goal oriented, you become enthusiastic. You don't have to drag yourself to cooking class as you dragged yourself to accounting class.

Now let us compare this example to ultra running. Ask yourself, "What does ultra running mean to me and what is my goal?" and "By meeting this goal, what joy will it bring into my life?" The answers will bring your running to a much deeper level. Maybe you're running an ultramarathon to be a role model for your children. Perhaps you've gone through some hardships and ultramarathon running is your vehicle for change. Or maybe you're running an ultramarathon to increase your self-confidence. Now you can earn that promotion or find that relationship you've always envisioned. After finishing an ultramarathon, what can't you accomplish?

Or maybe it's the self-transcendence experience that pulls you to such an extraordinary race. Perhaps you're looking to find a deeper meaning of life, one where creativity flows out of you like an abundant stream. You then use that creativity for your writing or artwork in a way that can serve others. The point is this: enthusiasm is powerful when running an ultramarathon. Think for a minute, have you ever considered where the word *enthusiasm* comes from? Enthusiasm comes from the Greek word *enthousiasmos,* meaning "Inspiration or possession by God." Inspired by God: need I say more?

Running an ultramarathon doesn't make us extraordinary human beings. What's extraordinary is what flows through us during these unfathomable bouts of human endurance. We transcend on the trails and then enter back into everyday life with much greater insight. Enthusiasm will propel you forward during an ultramarathon. It may appear stressful from the outside, but it's not. It's pure passionate intensity. Even when negative emotions arise, enthusiasm will quickly convert them to positive. Your "I can't" turns into "I can" and your hardships transform into opportunities to better your running—and your life.

Now, as I mentioned, when racing deep into an ultramarathon, especially 100 miles and longer, you may lose enthusiasm at some point. Eventually, your grand vision may shift from crossing the finish line to falling asleep. Some people will hold on longer than others. It all depends on the runner and what's genuinely driving them deep down.

To help, don't focus on the end goal of crossing the finish line, focus on the act of running. Try your best to stay in the present moment. Here's why: when you want to cross the finish line more than you want to be running, you become stressed. This extra resistance magnifies over the mileage. So make running in the present moment your main focus, not the finish line, and watch the life enter back into your stride. Otherwise, you'll fall out of enthusiasm. If so, the next stop on your mental map is enjoyment.

State #2: Enjoyment

When you run in the present moment during an ultramarathon, you step away from your past worries and the future finish line. Staying in the present moment increases your ability to enjoy the race. You don't have to ask yourself permission to enjoy the process of running. Don't ask yourself, "Can I really find enjoyment right now?" Asking similar questions will backfire. You develop reasons why you *can't* enjoy yourself instead. You start thinking, "My legs hurt" or "I'm out of energy" or "I'm tired" or "I'll train harder and enjoy the next race."

Well, here's the thing. The enjoyment for your next race won't come until you find enjoyment from running in the moment. Otherwise, you're experiencing a forward way of thinking. Forward-thinking stems from the common thought, "I will enjoy myself once I get to a certain point." For example, once you make X amount of money per year, *then* you will be happy. Or once you find the right partner, *then* your life will be complete. Or once you reach the finish line, *then* you will love running. We continuously look at tomorrow to bring us joy. But guess what? Tomorrow never comes when you're stuck in tomorrow. In this way, you can never appreciate today or the moment.

You may look for circumstances or people to bring you joy, and when they fall short, you may become disappointed or angry. We think if we lose the pounds, or find the spouse, or land the job, or earn the money, *then* we'll be happy. In a similar way, sometimes we believe that once we reach a certain mile *then* we'll enjoy the race. But here's the secret: It's not the physical act of running that brings joy on race day. What brings joy is the aliveness that flows through us and onto the course. We unleash our soul through every stride, and here lies the creation of true happiness.

This is one of the reasons I'm able to run so many ultramarathon races. Granted I am enthusiastic about reaching a new distance; however, after completing the 200-mile distance, I still run multiple shorter ultramarathons. Some days I go out and run a 50K training run with no food or water. On race day, the finish line isn't my focal point, because it's a means to an end. Alternatively, I become fully present and surrender to the journey. By letting go, I feel *alive*, and this is a power that no performance supplement could ever mimic.

Where Enjoyment Begins on Race Day

Enjoyment starts from the moment you open your eyes. On race day morning, practice gratitude before your ultramarathon begins. Wake up and say "thank you." Place your hands on your heart and focus on everything you are grateful for. Meditate on it. In a future chapter, I will outline a prerun meditation that helps increase energy, gain momentum, and enter into the present moment. But first, even before meditating, simply try finding appreciation in everything.

Be grateful for your legs that allow you to run anywhere at any time. Appreciate your heart, which beats every day without effort. Find the gratitude for the mystery of life and the chance to experience such a miraculous phenomenon. Express appreciation for your children, spouse, friends, parents, teachers, doctors, house, food, water, and the clothes on your back. For love, happiness, excitement, and passion. Whatever it is, feel *grateful*. Be thankful for the hardships since they are the lessons we learn that make us grow; they strengthen our souls for enduring the distance of an ultramarathon.

Gratitude will bring enjoyment into any ultramarathon. I also recommend practicing gratitude when the race begins. When I'm in the middle of a race, I constantly remind myself of how fortunate I am to be there. Running with strong legs, in the present moment, with a healthy pair of lungs, finding freedom on the course, and connecting with the trails . . . what's not to be grateful for? Plus, enjoyment instills aliveness; it drags you out of those race day lows. When you ride the wave of aliveness, running becomes effortless. It's in these moments when you find yourself feeling like it's mile 10 on mile 90.

Find Joy in the Moment

Practice bringing your awareness back to the present moment. When your mind wanders, readjust. Don't think, "I'll feel enjoyment once I'm on mile 95 and headed toward the finish line." Rather, feel joy in the moment, in this moment, in the present moment. Each time you forget your worries and find the NOW, you are training your mind to do so with less effort. In the present, the concept of time does not exist. It's here, in the stillness, in this timeless space where running 100- and 200-mile ultramarathons becomes possible. And who knows, maybe you are running them NOW.

Will you always find enjoyment in your races? What if you lose touch with enjoyment? What if one of your race-day lows becomes too low? Well, here is where you reach the last stop of the map. Here is where you tap into acceptance.

State #3: Acceptance

In mindful ultramarathon running, if you reach a part of the race where you can no longer enjoy yourself, at the very least, you can accept it. If you lose enthusiasm and enjoyment on race day, to continue running, *accept* your circumstances. Say to yourself, "For now, this is what I'm doing. I'm moving my feet forward, and I will continue to do so *willingly*."

The keyword here is *willingly*. By willingly accepting, you're still taking action, and this action will move you through the lows of an ultramarathon. For example, when I ran 100 miles in below freezing temperatures, it was ice-cold at night, and I could barely keep my eyes open. Running into the darkness, I was wet, cold, and tired. Because of this, I was unable to enjoy myself, and enthusiasm went out the window hours prior.

So what did I do? I *accepted* the situation and did so *willingly*. It was in this acceptance where I brought peace to my situation instead of irritation or hopelessness. That's even after it was so cold that my antichafing lubrication froze solid. If you are having trouble experiencing enthusiasm and enjoyment, which tend to dissipate at some point during an ultramarathon, then accept your circumstance.

The good news is you can stay in acceptance. You don't have to fall deeper if you apply a little effort. Any lower, and it's possible to DNF. Here's a tip: every time you begin to fall out of acceptance, focus on your feet. Don't ponder on where you've been or where you're headed, simply focus on putting one foot in front of the other . . . that's all. By placing attention on each stride, you bring your awareness back to the present moment. Now you can find enjoyment again in the race, and if you find enjoyment, then as you run closer to the finish line, you increase the chance of becoming enthusiastic again.

Understand that you can eliminate most of your suffering on race day by accepting the situation willingly. Remind yourself that you signed up for the race, you had a reason to complete it. Accept that, and you will prevent a DNF. Remember this: if you willingly suffer, you can run forever, but if you fall victim to suffering, you can hardly run at all. Choose to suffer, and the finish line will come.

Don't Create Suffering

So remember, by falling out of *acceptance, enjoyment,* or *enthusiasm* during an ultramarathon, you are adding an enormous amount of mental suffering on top of the already enormous amount of physical suffering. By staying in a state of acceptance, enjoyment, or enthusiasm, it will feel as if you're channeling a phenomenal form of energy to endure any level of physical suffering through the entire race. So follow your mental map, go through the motions, and stay in the present moment. Remind yourself that on the other side of the finish line is self-transcendence, and enthusiasm, enjoyment, and acceptance can get you there.

You now know how to run an ultramarathon with your mind as you continue on your mindful ultramarathon running journey. I know, struggle will always be around in your running. But remember, a runner's stamina is the result of all the struggles they are *willing* to overcome both inside and outside their running shoes. So get outside and use your new mental map to finish your next race while finding an appreciation for every moment.

CHAPTER 5:

Natural Powers

In ultramarathon running, it's common practice to look outside ourselves to find an edge. We look for a way to improve quickly, whether it's through something we ingest physically, like performance supplements, or mentally, like words of encouragement. In contrast, with mindful ultramarathon running, you realize that everything you could ever need is on the inside already.

It's true, you have natural powers available to you that come from within, not without. I will now reveal these powers. The only prerequisite is to be a human being. So unless you are wagging your tail as you read this, you are certainly qualified to possess the powers I speak of.

An Intro to Your Powers

I was soaring through the trails with a smile on my face and the sun on my back. The inspiration poured out from my soul—it felt unreal. The morning breeze was electrifying. I was unsure if the goose bumps shooting down my arms rose from the cool morning breeze or the new perception of the impossible transforming into my reality.

The final stretch of your first 100-mile ultramarathon is unexplainable. It's a uniquely gratifying journey. Your body and mind feel broken. Yet your spirit—yes, your glorious spirit—is still shining bright. The closer you get to the finish line, the less you can feel your legs. You would think the numbness was from the brutal beating of the last twenty-four hours of quad-crushing mileage, but it's not. Instead, it's from the intense joy that flushes through every cell of your being as you levitate to the end. In that sense, you don't run across the finish line of your first 100-mile ultramarathon, you float across it. That's the power of running from within, that's the power of the invincible human soul!

Is running a 100- or 200-mile ultramarathon easy? No, it's not. It's a rather challenging experience. Running an ultramarathon of this length takes a significant amount of training and dedication. But is it doable for you? Yes, it is. You are capable of more than you could ever imagine. As long as you have a beating heart, you can run any distance. It just takes patience in the journey, faith in the unknown, and a belief in your abilities.

You may have run 100 miles or longer already. But do you know what else helps you run longer? The answer: understanding some of the natural powers that are available to each of us. The fact is that we are human beings, we are born to run. After running over one hundred ultramarathon distances myself, including distances of 200 miles and longer, I can confidently say that running doesn't feel as much an act of achievement as it does a way of life. Human beings are runners, just like we are walkers, standers, and eaters.

Although running is natural for us, some take it to its extreme. Just look at some of the incredible bouts of human endurance that have taken place on our planet. Whether it's the runners who race in the Self-Transcendence 3100 Mile Race each year, or the hundreds of runners who have run across the United States. Or even running from a spiritual sense, like the Marathon Monks who run one thousand marathons in one thousand days.

As you can see, individuals from all sides of the globe are reaching far beyond their perceived limitations for all different reasons. If you take advantage of the powers available to you through mindful ultramarathon running, then you too will begin to see measurable results. Soon, running a longer distance transforms from a slight possibility to an absolute certainty. So read on for the natural powers available to you for reaching longer ultramarathon distances. Remember, if you keep reaching past your perceived limitations, outside your comfort zone eventually becomes the new inside, and what once seemed difficult is now what you do best.

The Power of Adaptation

How can someone go from running a schoolyard hill to climbing Mount Everest? How can a person go from barely getting out of bed in the morning, crippled from the stresses of life, to running their first marathon? How can someone like myself go from running a few miles on a treadmill to a 200-mile ultramarathon? What's the secret? Is it magic? No, far from it.

There are a few explanations, but what makes it physically possible is "adaptation." We, as human beings, are adaptation machines. We stress, heal, and grow back stronger to withstand new adversity. Because of this, I think it's fair to say that adaptation is quite possibly the genius of the human animal. It's survival.

An adaptation is a mutation, or genetic change, that helps living things survive in their environment. The adaptation can be physical (body) or behavioral (mind). What's the meaning for runners? It means that if you gradually increase your mileage, then you gradually adapt in both mind and body. Soon mile 20 feels like mile 10, and mile 30 feels like mile 20, and mile 50 feels less daunting. Simply put, the human body knows how to run longer, and it starts with adaptation.

Let's summarize: we're human beings, and as human beings we adapt to any and all changes and demands. The key here is "demand." We have to continually make progress if we truly want to take advantage of this power available to us, and that's where the second power comes in.

The Power of Progression

The word *progress* comes from the Latin word *progredi*, meaning to "walk forward and advance." It's a forward and onward motion. No, it doesn't have to be forced, but it does require *action*. Remember this: every one of your dreams is patiently sitting right outside your comfort zone. If you reach beyond your limitations, then guess what? Growth is a guarantee. And new limitations are created. In that sense, growth is a way of life. The renewal process is life as we invariably evolve, reproduce, and progress.

A person who wants to run an ultramarathon takes action. They put in the miles, and why not? If you aren't moving forward, then you're moving backward. Indeed, life is dynamic, it's far from static. If you're not becoming more enduring, you're becoming less enduring. If you're not becoming stronger, you're becoming weaker. And if you are not stepping outside your comfort zone regularly, then your comfort zone reduces in size.

Having hope for a brighter tomorrow provides us with more joy for a promising today. Progress is the lifeblood of ultramarathon running, and here's the good news: you can simply follow the running programs outlined in this book to progress to race day.

Generally speaking, a runner should progress their mileage only by approximately 10 percent each week. This way, you cover your mileage and run just far enough to grow but not so far as to do more harm than good (for example, injury or burnout). The training programs I offer in this book align with this rule. The programs are always here for you. The only question becomes whether you take action or not.

In addition, when discussing progress, I'm not only referring to running. Progress is essential in all aspects of training. Try to gain ground in everything you do. Jump out of bed faster each time before your run. Or make healthier choices more often. Or replace more of your energy-draining negative thoughts with more self-empowering positive thoughts. Here's the point: unless you progress, you'll digress, and you may not even realize it. If you make progress a constant, you'll find running goals come much easier. Why do they seem easier? The answer: *momentum*. That's your next power.

The Power of Momentum

Have you ever tried pushing a broken-down car? I have, I can think of a few occasions. In fact, one time I helped push a car off the road in the middle of a training run. Well, when you try pushing the car from a standstill, it takes a lot of energy. However, once it starts rolling, pushing becomes much easier. As long as you have momentum, it takes less energy.

So what happens if the car stops moving? When the car reaches a standstill, you're back to square one. Now it takes much more energy to get the tires rolling again. That's momentum. It's the force of strength gained by motion. And it doesn't only work for car tires; it works for running shoes as well. That's right, momentum also helps you increase running stamina.

Think about it. Have you ever gone on a run when you didn't feel up to it? If so, when you first start running, how do you feel? Usually not so great. But then you find your groove, and how do you feel then? Chances are you feel pretty good and your mindset does a complete one-eighty. Suddenly, you can't believe you didn't want to go for a run in the first place. It's here where moving forward becomes easier.

Now, what if you stop in the middle of your run and sit down to rest? Well, starting back up takes a substantial amount of energy. You lose momentum. As you may know, there's a saying in ultramarathon running: "beware of the chair." That's because if you sit down in the late stages of a 100-mile race, it becomes incredibly difficult to find the energy to start running again. Regardless, even with a pummeled pair of legs, once you get moving, you gain momentum. Now running feels relatively easier than it was when you first left the chair. I've been there many times—trust me. I remember sitting down to change my shoes at mile 150 in a 200-mile race. Starting back up was devastating. Yet, eventually, once I found my groove, it felt as if I had never stopped.

OK, so you may be thinking, "I get it, but it takes time to find that groove. The beginning of my run is always tough. Is there a way I can gain momentum faster?" And the answer is this: *absolutely*! To do so, consider "priming the pump." In other words, gain some momentum before your run. This prepares your body for ultra distances before leaving the house.

How do you "prime the pump"? Through a mindful ultramarathon running approach of course. To do so, close your eyes and perform a quiet meditation while focusing on your heart. Visualize all the things you're grateful for in your life. For more details, make your way over to the Balanced Program chapter, where I provide the steps for your prerun meditation. This doesn't have to be a time to consider all your accomplishments (although, feel free to do so!). It can be as simple as finding an appreciation for the warm morning sun on your face. Or a leaf on the tree outside. Or the clean drinking water that pours from your faucet.

Why does meditating on gratitude create momentum? Why does gratitude enhance your energy? First, it shifts your focus to the present moment. In the present moment, your past and future worries—which have the tendency to wear you down—vanish. Also, gratitude pulls you away from any possible disempowering stories you may live with and creates a new story of love and appreciation. That means no more excuses or self-limiting beliefs that prevent you from running longer or faster. And lastly, you'll find that gratitude improves your mood and increases your vibration.

"If you want to find the secrets of the universe, think in terms of energy, frequency, and vibration."

—Nikola Tesla

Here's the takeaway: after your gratification meditation, your pump is primed. You now have momentum, and you'll find your groove quicker. I enjoy meditating before every run and race. After a prerun meditation, when you start moving, it's like you've already been running for miles. You'll likely reach a heightened state where you align with the power of intention . . .

The Power of Intention

Our mind is an extraordinarily powerful tool. Yet what's most powerful is when we direct our focus. Remember what the old proverb tells us: "energy flows where attention goes." That's what setting an intention is all about. You declare a goal like running your first 100K or 100-mile race, but it takes setting an intention to wake up and run each training day to reach that goal.

Goals create guidance, intentions inspire action. How else could you reach your ultra running goals? There's a need for goal setting. However, goals keep your mind in the future. Setting an intention, on the other hand, is about directing your focus in the present moment toward your goals.

Have you ever set a goal so big that it became paralyzing? A goal with so many directions to choose from that you hesitated to take action and you became stuck in the world of contemplation without ever making any progress? Maybe that's what your ultramarathon journey feels like right now. If so, it's time to set an intention. Every intention you set is one step down the path toward your goal. Let the answers come to you through intuition, and when they do, set an intention and take inspired action.

When I set a goal to run in the morning and it's pouring rain, I may skip it. However, when I intend to run, there is no option, because I've already taken action. The moment I set the intention is the moment my run started, even if it was the night before. The rain is no more than extra resistance that has become part of my inevitable training run. Setting an intention is what propels your body into motion. Otherwise, the distance becomes nothing more than a dream that wanders in your mind.

So don't just set goals, set intentions, and watch your tremendous focus guide you to increasing your endurance. Setting an intention helps anchor your mind in the present moment, so your goals become easier to achieve. As does focusing on your breathing.

The Power of Breath

"Just breathe. . ." How many times have you heard these words? When you are panicking, just breathe." When you are exhausted, just breathe." When you are angry, just breathe."

Although we take approximately twenty thousand breaths per day, how often do we do so consciously? Consciously breathing helps you detach from your emotions while running. No longer are you a slave to your mind; now you are an observer of thought. This holds tremendous power when teaching your body how to run longer. Now instead of fighting that voice telling you to stop, you observe it. Instead of creating more resistance, you let go and run farther or hold a pace longer.

Ultramarathon running wears your body down. So it's critical to develop energy in any way possible. That's where deep breathing comes in. Here's the thing, breathing provides oxygen to your moving muscles, thus creating more energy for your runs. The more you focus on your breathing technique, the more energy you create. When you breathe deeply, it increases your oxygen supply; this in turn helps you run longer and faster.

Some experts say that most adults only use part of their lung capacity and say shallow breathing is a bad habit mainly developed from years of chronic stress and anxiety. The key is to breathe deep into your abdominals, not just your chest. If you've ever witnessed a baby sleeping, then you may have noticed them breathing in a similar fashion. If you look closely, you'll see their stomachs rise with each breath.

Breathing through the abdominal is our natural form and promotes the use of our lungs at full capacity. Plus, it's my understanding that deep breathing helps detoxify the body, relaxes the mind, and improves posture. Also, I read that it can strengthen the heart, lungs, and immune system, not to mention the positive effects it has on the nervous system.

Try it for yourself. From my own experience, deep breathing has boosted my energy levels and improved my running stamina. Mix that with how it can relieve unwanted tension, and you're on a direct path to one incredibly vibrant run. A run you enjoy, and a run you *love*.

The Power of Love

I started running ultra distances to achieve something great, and then, it led me to something much more profound. My pride transformed into gratification. It's been a humbling experience.

When I'm running deep into an unfathomable distance, I tap into something much larger than who we are or what we are. It's a natural flow, a flow of life—that flow is *love*. For the inner runner, for the spirit, for the soul, love is home. Union, love, togetherness—this is home. If you find love in your ultra running, then it departs from a goal-oriented process. The more you run, the more the ego breaks down, and the more you align with your soul's purpose.

In this sense, I don't run numerous ultramarathons to find achievement or because I'm addicted, I run because, well . . .

I'm home sick.

When you run with love, you find meaning in the miles and grace in your pace. Running ultramarathon distances doesn't necessarily get rid of your demons as much as it provides the courage to face them. Because on the other side of your darkest fears lies the light of your infinite power. That power is *love*.

How do you tap into it through your mindful ultramarathon running practice? Easy: let go. For some, however, running from a vulnerable state is emotionally uncomfortable. That's the ego. The ego wants to survive, and it loses its dominance as you detach from it. That's why it takes courage to surrender.

"We can easily forgive a child who is afraid of the dark; the real tragedy of life is when men are afraid of the light."

—Plato

No, it's not always easy to lead with love, and there's no perfectionism in letting go. Forcefully surrendering defeats its purpose. As a person who runs ultramarathons, I find that I dig much deeper within *myself* more than the *distance*. The distance I run outwardly is nothing more than a reflection of how deep I'm willing to go inwardly. So when finding love while running feels counterintuitive, or even a bit paradoxical, try to let go anyway.

"People are often unreasonable, illogical and self-centered . . .

. . . Forgive them anyway.

If you are kind, people may accuse you of selfish, ulterior motives . . .

. . . Be kind anyway.

If you are successful, you will win some false friends and some true enemies . . .

. . . Succeed anyway.

If you are honest and frank, people may cheat you . . .

. . . Be honest and frank anyway.

What you spend years building, someone could destroy overnight . . .

. . . Build anyway.

If you find serenity and happiness, they may be jealous . . .

. . . Be happy anyway.

The good you do today, people will often forget tomorrow . . .

. . . Do good anyway.

Give the world the best you have, and it may never be enough . . .

. . . Give the world the best you've got anyway.

You see, in the final analysis, it is between you and your God;

It was never between you and them anyway."

—Mother Theresa

The Power of Purpose

When will you know you are ready to run a longer ultramarathon? You won't. It takes a leap of faith. Signing up for a longer distance takes a jump into the unknown. Yes, the enthusiasm to start a training program helps, the determination to finish is useful, and the courage to reach the starting line makes things easier. However, standing at the starting line, I doubt you will feel ready. I never did.

Yet, if you think about it, isn't that true for anything new in life? I don't think it mattered how many baby books I read; I never felt 100 percent ready to be a parent. Then one day, my son was placed into my arms for the first time, and in a moment, parenthood made sense in its entirety. It's a natural occurrence. Some things are better learned experientially and these experiences take a leap of faith.

So when you jump into the unknown as a mindful ultramarathon runner, you begin to develop a profound knowledge that running is natural. It's part of the human experience. You realize it's no more complicated than moving your feet forward, and that learning how to run a longer ultramarathon comes instinctively. So have faith in your power and yourself, and whatever the distance, whatever the goal, whatever the intention . . . do it with *purpose*. Find your purpose and run with your heart.

CHAPTER 6:

Balanced Program

I decided to try yoga. I was looking for balance in my ultramarathon training program. I didn't know much about yoga, but I'm an ultra runner and I'm physically fit. Yoga should be easy, right? So I began. The first position: toe touch—*ouch*! The second position: kneel down . . . double *ouch*! The third position: sit on my insanely sore ultramarathon feet . . . OK, this isn't as easy as I thought.

You see, as an ultramarathon runner, I've married the long run. However, this union didn't start with a ceremony and champagne up in the air. Instead, it was a 100-mile race with extreme chafing down the pants. Yes, my cardiovascular endurance was at a peak level when I tried yoga for the first time. Yet I received a very honest lesson that day. I learned that you can have all the endurance in the world, but without balance in the body, you can find yourself in trouble. That's because if you are too one-sided, you create a blockage of energy. That's versus a circulating free flow of it.

Balancing Energy to Reach New Ultra Distances

Having excess energy in one part of the body creates a lack in another. This imbalance has the potential to promote injury, exhaustion, and prevent longevity in your ultramarathon training. On the contrary, with a balance of energy, that is, with energy that circulates freely and abundantly, you feel amazing. When this occurs, you have an incredible feeling of power that continually flows in your life, a feeling you will never want to give up.

Soon you'll start making changes naturally and without thought. You may take assertive action, such as wiping out processed foods completely from your eating regimen. No, not because you think it's healthy, but because you *know* it's healthy. You'll feel a new form of positive energy, and in a *massive* way.

This mindful approach to training was a big part of how I was able to endure multiple 200-mile ultramarathon training programs and races. Think about it: when preparing to run a 200-mile ultramarathon, considering the likelihood of finishing is not the only chance you take. You also have to risk the extra time and effort required to complete the ultramarathon training schedule. That's a whole lot of wasted time if you don't make it to race day.

Staying healthy and full of energy, both physically and mentally, is a *big* part of mindful ultramarathon running. Through the years, I've developed many successful practices to handle the excess mileage. As a husband and parent of three with a full-time career, I've learned how to fit ultra running into my life without burning out. It starts with following The Mindful Ultramarathon Running Training Program™.

A Quick Preview of the Program

Let's move along as I offer a useful guide to finding balance through different ultra distances. In fact, I provide training programs for the 50K, 50-mile, 100K, 100-mile, and 200-mile distances. The Mindful Ultramarathon Running Training Program™ is divided into five categories. Each part is listed below. Make sure you read every section from beginning to end and follow the running programs accordingly to make the most of my guidance.

Here are the five categories:

1. *Endurance: The Long Run*
2. *Muscular Strength: Weight Training*

3. *Flexibility and Balance: Yoga*
4. *Diet and Nutrition: Fat Adaptation*
5. *Mindfulness: Meditation*

Understand that finding the right balance for yourself is critical. How energized you feel on race day will be the difference between a DNF due to complete exhaustion and floating through the miles. As you may already know, popping quick hits of sugary supplements will only last so long. Eventually, as you start reaching 100- and 200-mile distances, you need to look inwardly for energy as well. Inside is where your true power lies.

My Journey to Longer Ultramarathon Distances

It's been quite a journey. First, I learned to run long, really, *really* long. This is the essence of ultramarathon running; this is what it's all about. To do so, I developed an ultramarathon training system for running any ultra distance by running only one day per week. I outline the entire program in my book *A Runner's Secret: One Run Will Get It Done.*

Second, I eliminated processed food, which drastically reduced nausea while running 100 miles, eventually leading to fat-adapted running. Although I touch on the subject in this book, I explain how you can easily become a fat-adapted runner in my book *The Fat Adapted Running Formula: A Step-By-Step Guide to Becoming a Fat Adapted Runner.* Later in this chapter, I will give you the secrets for transforming into a fat burning machine.

Third, I balanced my workouts with yoga, weightlifting, and bodyweight exercises. This provides an increase in strength, flexibility, and balance. Although I've weight trained for most of my life, things started really coming together once yoga was implemented into my weekly workout regime.

Lastly, I began performing a prerun meditation, mainly focusing on *gratitude.* As a result, I eliminated internal resistance (e.g., fear, worry, and self-doubt), providing more energy for the external resistance (running!). During a 100- or 200-mile race, you need all the energy you can hold on to.

I've destroyed my body on race day. So if you've been there, trust me, you're not alone. In fact, a lot of what I've learned in ultramarathon running has been through trial and error. My methods and anecdotes for nausea, chafing, sleep deprivation, exhaustion, and overall suffering on race day didn't come overnight. In the beginning, my running was all about pushing to the finish line with sheer grit and determination. One time I even collapsed and lost my memory completely for hours. I tell that story in a future chapter.

Today, I know the miraculous power in letting go and finding balance. As a result, I flow through the mileage of most races with minimum issues. Sure I still have my bad days, but they have reduced greatly. When your body isn't bogged down by processed foods or stiff from a lack of flexibility, you become lighter on your feet. Even more so, you gain a sensitivity to everyone and everything that provides energy, and that which takes it away.

You find an intimate connection with your breath because you feel the miracle of life flowing through you. By letting go and finding balance, you align with this life energy, and as a result, you can run astonishing distances. I really put this to practice during a seventy-two-hour race during which I ran over 200 miles.

On the morning of the race, I was full of energy. Then came the second night, when I could barely keep my eyes open. My groin and arms had been chafing for hours. I was wet, cold, tired, and hungry. At some point, I became fixated on the moon, praying it would make it across the sky for a new day and reset my internal clock and resurrect my broken body back from a race day grave.

Fortunately, over the years, I've learned quick bursts of energy when running ultramarathons is short-lived. After a while, the gels and blocks just don't cut it. It's more about a steady flow of sustainable energy. We are not burning paper here; it's not a sprint. We are burning coal here; it's an ultramarathon. So let go and find a balance (which you will learn from the programs), and align with a greater energy, the one from within.

Before we get into the guide, know this first: you will experience extra resistance when changing to The Mindful Ultramarathon Running Training Program™. The path up always begins down.

The Path Up Always Starts Down

I started a new summer job at a local bed and breakfast. On the first day I was given a shovel, wheelbarrow, and directions toward a field full of horse manure. You see, one of the tenants had been convicted and left his horses behind. In fact, the horses were left alone for months with no one cleaning up after them. My new boss said "Good luck!" and walked back into the office.

I thought to myself, "What kind of job is this?" "Is it worth my time?" "Should I leave?" I looked at the field, then looked at my car. The field . . . then back at my car . . . field . . . car . . . field . . . car . . . and just when I was about to say "forget it," rain began falling from the sky. No—it began pouring.

Did I quit? No. Surprisingly, the extra dose of adversity didn't push me to the edge of giving up. Instead, it motivated me. It was no longer a task at work, but instead, a test of my work ethic. As always, I was up for the challenge. I opened the gate and began cleaning.

Here's the point: I spent the whole day shoveling every square inch of manure off that field, and guess what? I never had to perform a task like that again. In fact, the rest of the summer was wonderful. The owner left me alone to manage the maintenance of the entire property. He left the scheduling up to me. It was the best summer job I ever had as a kid.

I gained two insights from that experience. First, most anything worth doing in life takes two steps backward before you can take three steps forward. Just like your muscles expand by demand, you must travel down before you can go up—sadly, most of the time, people quit before enjoying the fruits of their labor. Secondly, I can never utter the following words again: "At least I never had to shovel sh*t for a living."

Don't Give Up on the Program

When you first become a runner, you feel enthusiasm, eagerness, and aliveness. However, once things become tougher—which they often do—a positive running experience can turn negative . . . and *fast*.

Here's where many people give up on their dreams of running an ultramarathon. They give up because of the relatively enormous amount of resistance upfront. However, they likely don't know the secret of the endurance world. The secret I'm referring to is *momentum*, and once you gain momentum, things become much, *much* better.

So how do you prevent giving up? To start, try to view the subjective mind objectively. Remember, it's your thoughts that create emotions, and those emotions can be a clue to what's going on in your subconscious mind. As I like to say, "the mind is the most powerful tool you have during your ultramarathon training program." As a result, you can develop the emotional intelligence to readily withstand the physical adversity. That's because you align with the nature of knowing there's opportunity hidden in every aspect of resistance. When this happens, suddenly, your life flips upside down and the once-old stressful world you lived in becomes a new magical place you call home.

Enjoy the Ultramarathon Climb

Once you work through the many different running issues, usually through trial and error (hydration, gear, chafing, etc.), you can develop your own unique process, a process tailored to *your body* and *your* mind. You no longer focus on what you "should" do and instinctively know what your body needs. Now you can scale the process to longer distances like 100 and 200 miles while making different tweaks along the way.

The sad truth is that some runners give up well before experiencing the freedom of being an enduring runner. That is, one who has the ability to run miles upon miles without stopping, along with the joy and happiness that comes with crossing the finish line on race day. That's why I write: to help guide and inspire others to keep moving forward toward their running goals. You see, there's so much power in setting an intention, yet we can easily find ourselves lost, wishing on a star instead. So remember, it's about bringing presence into your run, not leaving it mentally trapped in the eternal thoughts of a future finish. When you become lost in the future on race day, you suffer.

Here's the good news: when you accept the suffering, you can transcend the pain. Do this, and every mile becomes a miracle. By staying in the present moment, you'll avoid pitfalls along your journey. As you may know already, an ultramarathon is a tough mountain to climb. Yet sooner or later, you'll get to the top of that mountain. You'll look out into the vast horizon, and guess what? You'll see more mountains, choose one, and then start climbing again.

If you're reading this as an ultra runner, I'm guessing you already knew this because you likely have multiple finishes under your belt. Don't ever forget that true happiness rarely comes from the view at the peak of the mountain and almost always from the progressive journey of the climb.

Before we get started, allow me to offer one more piece of advice. The secret to never giving up on The Mindful Ultramarathon Running Training Program™ is to *always take one more step*. Ultra running is filled with adversity that challenges you both physically and mentally in every way. It won't be easy, but it will be possible. You are more enduring than you could ever imagine.

The Mindful Ultramarathon Running Training Program *TM*

Now, let's start the program. Keep reading for a breakdown of The Mindful Ultramarathon Running Training Program™. Remember, I provide training programs for the 50K, 50-mile, 100K, 100-mile, and 200-mile distances.

To clarify, this program isn't about balance in terms of even proportion. As an ultra runner, of course the long run is going to be your primary focus. The different exercises and practices will support your efforts in becoming more enduring. All body parts rely intricately on one another for support. If one particular body part is neglected, another part suffers.

Finding the right balance is necessary to staying healthy and energized during your ultramarathon training program. Let's begin!

1—Endurance: The Long Run

In the following training programs, your weekly long run is your main focus. Remember, we are not looking for a program of even proportion here, instead, it's about finding a unique balance between endurance, strength, flexibility, balance, nutrition, and mindfulness to support your mindful ultramarathon running lifestyle. Your weekly long run is building your endurance. There are two types of endurance: *cardiovascular and muscular.* I will briefly explain both.

First, *cardiovascular endurance is* how efficiently your heart can provide oxygen to muscles during prolonged physical activity. Second, *muscular endurance* is the ability of a muscle to continuously exert force against resistance over a long period of time. Running covers both cardiovascular and muscular endurance. As an ultra runner, you should use both.

There is no need to cross-train with other endurance-building exercises. However, in this program, you will perform alternative exercises to achieve balance; that is, to prevent burnout and support your running body during training. As a result, you will likely be less sore, feel healthier, and be more energized than ever before. Your energy will flow freely and you'll feel a miraculous increase in alertness.

With this program, you will run only two days per week. One long run and one recovery run on tired legs. The runs are back-to-back. This simulates running with "dead legs," which commonly occurs on ultramarathon race day.

I've personally trained and raced every standard ultra distance by running only *one* day per week, as I explain in my book *A Runner's Secret: One Run Will Get It Done.* Other times I trained for every standard ultra distance by running *two* days per week. Now, whether I run one or two days is based on my schedule and the balance of my energy. So this time around, I'll share each *two*-day schedule with you. If you live a super busy life, which I can relate to as a parent, these programs could be the answer to your running prayers.

Yes, you can run extraordinarily long distances by running only two days per week. I've taken this program up to the 200-mile distance and I still use it today. As I've said in my other books, it's about *finding the greatest maximum results in the shortest period of time*. The following programs will deliver results.

The Long Run Weekly Recommendation: one long run followed by one recovery run.

WEEK	MON	TUE	WED	THU	FRI	SAT	SUN
	The Mindful Ultramarathon Running 50K Training Program™						
1	Weight Training	Yoga	Weight Training	Yoga	Rest	7	4
2	Weight Training	Yoga	Weight Training	Yoga	Rest	8	4
3	Weight Training	Yoga	Weight Training	Yoga	Rest	9	4
4	Weight Training	Yoga	Weight Training	Yoga	Rest	9	5
5	Weight Training	Yoga	Weight Training	Yoga	Rest	10	6
6	Weight Training	Yoga	Weight Training	Yoga	Rest	11	6
7	Weight Training	Yoga	Weight Training	Yoga	Rest	12	7
8	Weight Training	Yoga	Weight Training	Yoga	Rest	14	7
9	Weight Training	Yoga	Weight Training	Yoga	Rest	7	4
10	Weight Training	Yoga	Weight Training	Yoga	Rest	5	3
11	Weight Training	Yoga	6	Yoga	5	Rest	4
12	Rest	Rest	Rest	Rest	Rest	Rest	**RACE**

*Recommendation: complete the 50K training program before beginning the 50-mile training program.

The Mindful Ultramarathon Running 50-Mile Training Program™							
WEEK	**MON**	**TUE**	**WED**	**THU**	**FRI**	**SAT**	**SUN**
1	Weight Training	Yoga	Weight Training	Yoga	Rest	11	6
2	Weight Training	Yoga	Weight Training	Yoga	Rest	12	7
3	Weight Training	Yoga	Weight Training	Yoga	Rest	14	7
4	Weight Training	Yoga	Weight Training	Yoga	Rest	15	8
5	Weight Training	Yoga	Weight Training	Yoga	Rest	16	9
6	Weight Training	Yoga	Weight Training	Yoga	Rest	18	9
7	Weight Training	Yoga	Weight Training	Yoga	Rest	20	10
8	Weight Training	Yoga	Weight Training	Yoga	Rest	22	12
9	Weight Training	Yoga	Weight Training	Yoga	Rest	11	6
10	Weight Training	Yoga	Weight Training	Yoga	Rest	8	5
11	Weight Training	Yoga	8	Yoga	7	Rest	6
12	Rest	Rest	Rest	Rest	Rest	Rest	**RACE**

*Recommendation: complete the 50-mile training program before beginning the 100K training program.

WEEK	MON	TUE	WED	THU	FRI	SAT	SUN
	The Mindful Ultramarathon Running 100K Training Program™						
1	Weight Training	Yoga	Weight Training	Yoga	Rest	14 _22.5_	7
2	Weight Training	Yoga	Weight Training	Yoga	Rest	15 _24_	8
3	Weight Training	Yoga	Weight Training	Yoga	Rest	17 _27_	9
4	Weight Training	Yoga	Weight Training	Yoga	Rest	18 _29_	10
5	Weight Training	Yoga	Weight Training	Yoga	Rest	20 _32_	11
6	Weight Training	Yoga	Weight Training	Yoga	Rest	22 _35_	12
7	Weight Training	Yoga	Weight Training	Yoga	Rest	24 _38.5_	13
8	Weight Training	Yoga	Weight Training	Yoga	Rest	28 _45_	14
9	Weight Training	Yoga	Weight Training	Yoga	Rest	14 _22.5_	7
10	Weight Training	Yoga	Weight Training	Yoga	Rest	10 _16_	6
11	Weight Training	Yoga	12	Yoga	9	Rest	7
12	Rest	Rest	Rest	Rest	Rest	Rest	**RACE**

Recommendation: complete the 100K training program before beginning the 100-mile training program.

WEEK	MON	TUE	WED	THU	FRI	SAT	SUN
	*The Mindful Ultramarathon Running 100-Mile Training Program*™						
1	Weight Training	Yoga	Weight Training	Yoga	Rest	22	12
2	Weight Training	Yoga	Weight Training	Yoga	Rest	24	13
3	Weight Training	Yoga	Weight Training	Yoga	Rest	27	14
4	Weight Training	Yoga	Weight Training	Yoga	Rest	29	16
5	Weight Training	Yoga	Weight Training	Yoga	Rest	32	17
6	Weight Training	Yoga	Weight Training	Yoga	Rest	35	19
7	Weight Training	Yoga	Weight Training	Yoga	Rest	40	20
8	Weight Training	Yoga	Weight Training	Yoga	Rest	44	23
9	Weight Training	Yoga	Weight Training	Yoga	Rest	22	12
10	Weight Training	Yoga	Weight Training	Yoga	Rest	16	9
11	Weight Training	Yoga	19	Yoga	15	Rest	11
12	Rest	Rest	Rest	Rest	Rest	Rest	**RACE**

Recommendation: complete the 100-mile training program before beginning the 200-mile training program.

WEEK	MON	TUE	WED	THU	FRI	SAT	SUN
1	Weight Training	Yoga	Weight Training	Yoga	Rest	25	12
2	Weight Training	Yoga	Weight Training	Yoga	Rest	17	8
3	Weight Training	Yoga	Weight Training	Yoga	Rest	28	15
4	Weight Training	Yoga	Weight Training	Yoga	Rest	20	7
5	Weight Training	Yoga	Weight Training	Yoga	Rest	35	20
6	Weight Training	Yoga	Weight Training	Yoga	Rest	25	10
7	Weight Training	Yoga	Weight Training	Yoga	Rest	45	20
8	Weight Training	Yoga	Weight Training	Yoga	Rest	25	18
9	Weight Training	Yoga	Weight Training	Yoga	Rest	60	20
10	Weight Training	Yoga	Weight Training	Yoga	Rest	35	15
11	Weight Training	Yoga	Weight Training	Yoga	Rest	Rest	25
12	Weight Training	Yoga	17	Yoga	Rest	Rest	13
13	Weight Training	Yoga	7	Yoga	Rest	Rest	5
14	Rest	Rest	Rest	Rest	Rest	Rest	**RACE**

The Mindful Ultramarathon Running 200-Mile Training Program™

*Recommendation: grab a space suit; you have just left planet earth.

2—Muscular Strength: Weight Training

The strength training section of this program will likely bring focus to areas of your body that don't receive enough attention. Increasing your core strength is a game-changer as an ultra runner. Muscular strength will support your efforts in running longer. Building a strong body will prevent slouching from fatigue on race day and may even help prevent common running injuries along the way.

So what exactly is muscular strength anyway? Muscular strength is the maximum amount of force a muscle can exert in a single contraction. Yes, it's possible to improve muscular strength and endurance at the same time, as some strength training will support your running body. Especially when you take your ultramarathon training to the trails.

Strength training 2–3 days per week is adequate. To do so, perform a full body workout alternating between push and pull exercises. Play around with the amount of exercises and repetition. I recommend always progressing. Here are three ways to progressively train with weights:

- Same weight, increase repetitions (e.g., 5 sets of 100 lbs. at 6-7-8-9-10 reps)
- Increase weight, same repetitions (e.g., 5 sets of 80-85-90-95-100 lbs. at 5 reps each)
- Increase weight, increase repetitions. (e.g., 5 sets of 80-85-90-95-100 lbs. at 6-7-8-9-10 reps)

Please note, for this program, only weight train legs once per week. Make sure it's the beginning of the week. For example, if you run on Saturday and Sunday, weight train your legs on the following Monday or Tuesday. All other weight training that week should be upper body only.

Personally, I weight train my upper body a few times per week. On Monday, I sometimes strength train my legs. For example, leg presses, dumbbell squats, lunges, calf raises, etc. But again, I do so sparingly. I've spent years ultramarathon training without weight training my legs entirely. If you're attempting to reach a *new* distance, you can do the same. Feel it out and choose the level of leg training that's best for you.

It's worth noting that I may do a strength yoga session the following Tuesday or Wednesday, but that's it. If I train with weights on Thursday and/or Friday, it's only my upper body. If it's race week, I perform no leg workouts whatsoever and keep my yoga light.

Weekly Weight Training Recommendation: 1–2 days full body (legs optional)

3—Flexibility and Balance: Yoga

Flexibility is the range of motion in your joints, while *balance* is the ability to stay in control of body movement. I have found that performing exercises that increase flexibility and balance can improve endurance and prevent injury. That's because a new bending body is less stiff. In other words, your lower body has a wider range of motion.

As you can imagine, this is exceedingly beneficial for those who prefer trail ultramarathons. Those sharp turns, hidden rocks, and raised tree roots can wreak havoc on your feet, ankles, and legs if you're not careful. Improving flexibility and balance is another line of defense as you strengthen your trail legs. Eventually, you'll increase coordination and agility as well. This is best done through yoga.

Yoga simply means "union" and is a practice of bodily postures, breath control, and simple meditation. No, you don't have to become a yogi to gain its benefits. Through consistent yoga practice, you learn to let go of internal resistance and become more receptive to life energy.

There are many different styles and techniques when it comes to yoga, so it will take some experimenting on your part. But you know what? That's the journey of yoga. You fall into your own style based on how you feel, and your practice becomes an expression of your being.

So find an at-home beginner yoga program or join a class. Choose whichever feels most comfortable. Yoga is a practice, not a sport. It's process focused, not results driven. In a like manner, stretching is about sensation, not destination. For this purpose, take your time and have fun! By following a yoga program, your flexibility and balance will naturally improve. Yoga can provide longevity in your running—and your life.

Weekly Yoga Recommendation: 2 sessions per week. Perform any strength yoga sessions early in the week.

4—Diet and Nutrition: Fat Adaptation

Next, consider not only what you are putting into your body, but also your outlook on food in general. Here I will offer a possibly different approach to your current eating habits. So let's take it to the kitchen . . .

Please note, this section is not intended to promote any kind of belief structure or so-called diet. I am not a certified nutritionist and make no claims to the contrary. You are ultimately responsible for all decisions pertaining to your health. Remember, sometimes when you push the limits, the limits push back. So, proceed with caution and never forget that safety comes first.

Have you ever heard someone say, "Are you still on your diet?" Do you see what's wrong with that question? By "going on a diet," we declare that our poor eating habits are the norm. It's like going on a vacation only to eventually return home. In this way, diets are a trap, and they require a paradigm shift to escape.

Here's a new perspective for you: We are real, live people who require real food so our bodies can function the right way. When our bodies function correctly, we are healthy; when they don't, we are not healthy. A healthy body is an energized body that metabolizes efficiently. This is essential for ultramarathon running. Here's another way to say it: a healthy runner's body is one who eats healthy—and to eat healthy is to eat real food. The rest will take care of itself. Plus, the cleaner you eat, the less energy is required for digestion.

Personally, I eat as close to the source as possible. Over a decade ago, I cut out grains and dairy. A few years back, I stopped eating meat as well. By eliminating processed foods, your body detoxifies itself. You become more sensitive to what provides energy, and what takes it away. Once you get a taste of a real healthy lifestyle, you will never want go back.

Eventually, you only choose to consume foods that cleanse your body, not those that clog it. There's power in plants, but I've noticed that you need to cleanse your body to feel the magic. To sum it up: eat clean to increase energy levels for ultramarathon training. Do this while running, and something interesting will begin to happen. When you keep your sugars low, you may start to transform into a fat-adapted runner.

What is fat adaptation? The process of fat adaptation refers to moving your body's primary energy source from glucose (sugar) to fatty acids (fat). When this occurs, your body stops depending on sugars (carbs) and prefers fat as fuel instead. Your body becomes far more efficient in burning its own stored fat as fuel and is less dependent on sugar. Low sugar, in a perfect world, means no sugar crash, no constant replenishment, and no sugar addiction. Just a continuous flow of sustainable energy, available to you always. This comes in handy during periods of prolonged running.

When your body is efficient at burning fat as fuel, you can run longer without needing to refuel because the fuel comes from within. Fat adaptation is the body's preferred metabolic state. That's what our bodies are designed to do. We eat, store fat, and use it for energy later.

Burning fat is like burning coal: slow and steady, burning and burning for a long time. Conversely, sugar is like lighter fluid, a quick flash, then *poof*—it's gone. So, when you're trying to reach longer distances, especially ultramarathon distances, which type of fire do you want to burn?

Although I won't get into all the details of fat-adapted running in this book, I will provide my secret as promised. Next to removing grains, the most effective step that helped me become a fat-adapted runner came from running on *empty*. That's right, no prerace meals, no consumption midrun, nothing. This is in combination with your new high-fat/low-carb healthy eating habits. That's also assuming you're not drinking sugary beverages like soda.

Here's the process for running on empty:

1. Wake up early in the morning.
2. Drink a glass of water.
3. Go run.

There's a magnificent beauty in simplicity, wouldn't you agree? You then increase the mileage of your next run, which increases the distance you run on empty. That's it! Since you have The Mindful Ultramarathon Running Training Program™, you can perform each run on empty if you'd like to work on becoming a fat-adapted runner yourself.

Weekly Fat Adaptation Recommendations: Practice intermittent fasting. Eat nuts in the afternoon, and one large meal for dinner that is rich in vegetables and essential oils. Run on empty for greater results.

5—Mindfulness: Meditation—Mind, Body, and Soul

Be open to receiving. Accept this section as a gift. Let go and relax into a prerun meditation. Allow this meditation to last ten to fifteen minutes in length. Focus on eliminating internal resistance, increasing energy, and settling into the present moment. Don't force it like a sprint. Plug into it like a network. Find your home deep within the stillness.

We place so much emphasis on the visible world, yet everything material was once an invisible thought waiting to be born. It's about finding the right sequence and bringing it to life. Think about it. Every word I'm writing in this book is already in use somewhere else. No, not in the same sequence or with the same intention. However, every single word was spoken or written many times since the English language began. In that sense, I did not invent the words, but instead, discovered the sequence. I pieced sentences together inside the invisible world and brought them to the visible one. I transferred each sentence from thought to material.

We are all creators. Our creations happen both consciously and unconsciously. We create art and literature, buildings and statues, laws and guidelines, thoughts and excuses, dreams and nightmares. So make an intention to create a great run, and allow your feet to be the brush strokes of a running masterpiece. Then, use these creative powers to your advantage during a prerun mediation.

Think about it, if you can think yourself sick, then why not well? If you can think yourself sad, then why not happy? And if you can think yourself into a bad run, then why not a good run? Why not into the best run of your life? The point is this: if you can think of yourself as a 200-mile ultra runner, then you can become one.

Sure it will take time. Any peak you scale starts at the base of the mountain. I know. I've been there. I went from running a few miles on a treadmill to running over 200 miles in one race. So here's the truth: the same runner in you is the same runner in me and it's my pleasure to help guide you on your mindful ultramarathon running journey.

Ever forget you are running? Time disappears, does it not? And miles feel like minutes. It's like magic. As I like to say: The moment I forget I'm running is the moment my soul takes the wheel. I don't know where I'm headed, but I know it's a beautiful destination.

So focus on a ten- to fifteen-minute meditation once or twice per day. One in the morning and one before any run. You can find a short guide on meditation yourself, or follow the one provided next.

The Mindful Ultramarathon Running Meditation

Keep reading as I briefly explain how to perform your prerun meditation.

PREPARATION: Sit in a quiet, dark room. Find a place without interruption; a place where you'll feel comfortable and safe. Play a little soft meditative music in the background if you like.

Next, find a comfortable position. You can sit with legs crossed on the floor, against a wall, in a chair, or you can lie down. Again, comfort is key. Once you settle in, place your hands palms-up on your knees or crossed in your lap. Close your eyes and keep them shut for the rest of the meditation. Although I list times for each part, the minutes are only a point of reference. During your meditation you can relax and let it flow.

PART 1: Breath for one to two minutes. Take deep breaths in through the nose and out through the mouth. Acknowledge thoughts that come in without judgment and let them pass.

PART 2: Express gratitude for three minutes. Spend time thinking of all the things you appreciate in life.

Here's the good news: there's so much to be grateful for! At first, you may feel some resistance. However, the more you practice gratitude, the easier it becomes. After a while, you will replace your expectations with gratification and reach an unlimited mindset.

I can't help but feel grateful for a new morning. The gift of living another day is a blessing and I can't think of a better way to celebrate than to run. Here's the thing: gratitude will eliminate the internal resistance, so you have more energy for the external resistance. Because if you're looking for pain and misery while running . . . you'll find it, and if you're looking for joy and happiness while running, you'll find it. Remember the saying: "energy flows where attention goes."

PART 3: Heal yourself for three minutes. With your eyes still closed, picture a radiant light coming down from the sky above. As it penetrates the top of your head, give thanks for the healing you receive in each part of your body. If there's a particular spot that's bothersome, focus on it, and express infinite gratitude.

PART 4: Spend one to three minutes giving back. To do so, send out the same healing energy to those you love, know, or that you are intuitively guided toward. Consider it a blessing.

Have you been holding a grudge against someone? A heavy heart will only cause greater stress and resistance while running. So forgive them, bless them, heal them, and let it go. When you forgive others, you heal yourself. Your outer world is a reflection of your inner world. Create a beautiful place on the inside, and the outside takes care of itself. You become more positive and attract even more positive situations. No longer do you run in a way that it "should be," you run in a way that it "could be." To prevent your dreams from shriveling up dead, keep your eye on the magic ahead.

PART 5: Visualize for one to two minutes.

If it's the beginning of the day, visualize a life goal. Or if it's before your run or race, visualize how well it's going to go. As you gain energy during your prerun meditation, it will feel as if you already caught your groove. This eliminates a great deal of resistance or hesitation up front.

As stated, a prerun meditation creates momentum. Crawl, then walk, then run, then fly! Find the momentum, let go of limitations, and set your spirit free! To know nothing is to know everything, and to let go is to fly. So surrender to move forward. That's how you run a new distance, that's how you run for 100 miles without stopping!

As I like to say: The first 50 miles I rely on my body and run on the trail. The next 40 miles I rely on my head and run in the mind. The last 10 miles I rely on my heart and run in the sky. When you accept the suffering, you can transcend the pain. Do this, and every mile becomes a miracle. For me, an ultramarathon is not an athletic competition, but instead, a spiritual journey. I let go to move forward, falling upward with every step.

PART 6: Right before you end your meditation, Ask yourself this question: "How could I ever run out of energy, if I am energy?!"

Do this, and you will be intuitively led through the door of unimaginable distances.

Remember, the power doesn't lie in the visible representation of these words, but it does exist in the invisible appreciation of your thoughts. Give thanks every time you run, and watch what running gives back in return.

Running Watchless

A few years ago, I was traveling toward the beach for a summer vacation on the East Coast of the United States. On the car ride there, I jumped out 37 miles from my destination. At the time, this was my longest attempted distance for a training run. Ultra running was still new to me, and everything was going well until around mile 28. All of a sudden, I began to lose it! My eyes became glued to my watch and every minute seemed like an eternity until I eventually started to walk. I felt like a slave to the digital countdown of time.

Enough was enough. I took off the GPS watch attached to my wrist and launched it as far as my arm would allow it. You see, I learned something about myself that day. That day, I learned that monitoring my time, splits, and pace while running did not motivate me—actually, it did the exact opposite. For me, checking my pace over and over again added an extra weight on my shoulders. Monitoring my running through a watch beat me down mentally. Losing the watch helps me stay in the present moment and to continue moving forward on race day. I lose track of how much farther I have left, so I just continue running. Ultimately, there's never been a finish line but a continuous journey to travel.

The point: losing the watch was one of the best decisions I have ever made. You may want to consider doing the same. This way you focus on the process, not the results, because it's here where real progress is made.

Start Your New Journey

It's challenging, going to bed at 9:00 p.m. only to sleep for an hour and a half. Then waking up at 10:30 p.m. to run 30 miles before work. I don't take running to its extremes only to become better myself, I also do it to gain greater insight and more experience to share with others.

I don't try to write cleverly; I try to write authentically. A witty statement is entertainment in the moment, but a paradigm shift can be a blessing for life. By doing so, I hope I can help you reach a running goal that you hold close to your heart.

Mindful ultramarathon running has changed my life in so many positive ways. It only feels right to turn around and lift the next person up. As an ultramarathon runner, there is one constant that matters more than every other: mindfulness.

Ultramarathon running is an inside job. If you are happy with yourself, you will be happy with your running. You can get caught up running from the outside-in, pushing your body through each run, only to burn out. Or you can run from the inside-out, eliminate internal resistance, and let your inner runner free! That requires patience. That requires balance. That requires the act of letting go.

Ultra running takes a lot of time and energy. Allow your outer results to be a product of your inside work. The miles you travel inwardly will allow you to travel more miles outwardly. If I can recommend any way to get started, it's through The Mindful Ultramarathon Running Training Program™.

Now that you have a path to run longer and stronger, you may be asking yourself, what about faster? As fate would have it, while writing this book, I was intuitively led to a way of running faster mindfully through an approach that works in my mindful ultramarathon running practice and a way that will work for you.

CHAPTER 7:

Run Faster

In mindful ultramarathon running, it's much more meaningful to work on creating an unbreakable mind and body, as opposed to chasing a placement or time. I think to myself, "Why compete when you can create?" Separation surely reduces energy, while togetherness increases it exponentially.

Even so, competition doesn't have to be exclusionary. In fact, it's quite inclusive. Consider this: the meaning of the word *compete* is "to strive for an objective," and it comes from the Latin word *competere* meaning to "strive together." So, when we compete, we strive together to reach an objective or goal. Racing one another creates more resistance for greater growth.

Whether you decide to compete or not on race day, there's one constant: *you will struggle*. Sure, the techniques I've developed for handling suffering have benefited my running. After a while, you learn what to do with the pain. I expected this lesson. However, what I did not expect was how I've been able to use these same running practices to improve my everyday life.

That's why fast times, first-place finishes, and new personal bests have never sat very high on my ultramarathon priority list. Although I've placed in races, that's only been a reflection of how well I can handle suffering on race day by doing things such as fasting for an entire 50K or practicing staying in the present moment or running while finding a more profound insight for life.

For a while, my ultra running goal was to see how long I could run before feeling bad by preventing and handling nausea and exhaustion, self-doubt, hopelessness, soreness and fear. In general, I rarely ever run at what most would consider a "fast" ultramarathon pace. Well, until recently . . .

You see, during a recent ultramarathon, I developed a deep insight that created a paradigm shift. I aligned with a knowledge that stuck with me for the entire 50 miles. The idea was simple, effective, and somewhat liberating. Here was my thought: set an intention for every step. In addition, each painful step became a sacrifice. It was a thank-you for something greater, for the miracle of life. In this way, not only did I run faster than usual, I transcended the pain. Plus, this focus brought awareness to *every* effort, keeping my mind in the present moment. No suffering from obsessing over the future finish line.

There were times I considered running faster, allowing the ego to creep in. However, something kept telling me to trust the process instead. To continue intending to take every step. That's it. Focusing your mental energy on each stride guides your body forward placing you in the right position to perform at maximum efficiency.

I don't wear GPS watches. I run on feel. So I paid attention to each step and the result was I ran my fastest 50-mile ultramarathon ever, and most important, I developed a mindful approach in how to run faster with less effort, a method I can now share with you in this book.

How to Run Faster Mindfully

As I've mentioned, increasing speed has never been my main focus. However, being mindful and feeling good during every ultramarathon has been. Because of this, naturally, my times have improved. Think about it, if you want to feel better, you'll make many changes. How often you run, what you eat, the books you read, it all contributes to a better race experience.

As of late, not wasting any steps because of a genuine appreciation for life has made me faster. Indeed, if you run with intention, your speed will increase. Remember, a 1 percent increase for three runs is not 3 percent. Your improvement compounds. Each time you run faster or boost stamina, you're building from the new you. That is, a new runner who is faster and more enduring. This mindful approach keeps the ego out to prevent burnout and allows your mind to find the present moment thus improving speed. Rest assured, I will explain each in more detail.

When I crossed the finished line of the race, I snapped out of a *trance*. It was a mental shift. To help you do the same, let's dig a little deeper. Continue reading as I explain each part of learning how to run faster mindfully.

1. Let Go for more energy
2. Give a consistent effort to increase speed
3. Run in the present moment to avoid suffering
4. Transcend pain to prevent slowing down
5. Detach from the ego to avoid burnout
6. Run while fasting to run forever

Let's begin. Continue reading as we discuss the art of letting go. You will soon understand how to align with a natural energy and distinguish between an even effort and running too fast.

1. Let Go for More Energy

Through the countless commercials, news clips, and gossip columns, we've become hypnotized by certain beliefs. Quite possibly, the most dangerous of these beliefs is that we should feel good all the time. We're persuaded to believe if we feel negative in any way then, well, something is wrong with us. This is the most untrue promise of our existence.

So we numb our pain with some magic pill filled with empty promises, only to suppress our emotions. As you likely know, stacking unresolved feelings can be dangerous. With enough pressure, the negativity adds up, becoming too heavy to handle. Anxiety disorders, angry outbursts, and deep depression are only the start.

Therein lies the truth: life is not about feeling good all the time. Life's about the highs and the lows. That's growth. We break down, stress, and grow. Avoiding the lows will stunt your growth. That's how we learn. Take developing your mental muscles, for example. Fear is the internal weight in the gym of your mind. Run away from your fears, and your mind becomes fragile. Run toward your fears, and your mind becomes stronger—and it takes a mightier mind to run an ultramarathon.

Although I'm a believer in positive thinking, there's no positivity without negativity. The natural flow of life is not up-up-up-up or down-down-down. It's up-down-up-down. That's why when you direct your focus toward a specific goal, you grow stronger, reaching new highs. But the lows will be there.

We go through seasons. Like summer to fall, life comes and goes. Just like the flowers that bloom each spring, we live and we die, along with the worms in the ground, the leaves on the trees, and the stars in the sky. Take your muscles, for example. In building muscle, you have to struggle if you want to grow. We expand by demand. As a runner, you must go through resistance if you want to run longer, stronger, and faster.

Here's the point, although you can't completely escape the highs and lows, you can transcend the pain. Because oddly enough, it's inside of struggle where you find the reward. It's inside of negativity where positivity lives. It's inside of darkness where you discover the most radiant light. What a paradox life can be.

Like the old saying goes, "two steps forward, one step backward." To go up, you must first go down. This is not hyperbole or some positive thinking cliché. This is a law that governs our lives. As an ultra runner, on race day, it's easy to identify with these highs and lows. Through such repetition, one can get trapped in their compulsive cycle of thought. But here's the good news: If you learn to let go, you can align with the flow of life. When this occurs, you'll feel a new level of energy that you never knew existed.

Become the observer, not the thinker on race day. Let someone else track your time as you run from timelessness. This way, you are not the mind, but instead, use it as a tool.

We must go down to go up.

Travel through hell to make it to heaven.

Expand by demand.

Forget yourself to remember who you really are.

Let go to move forward.

Or, one of my personal favorites, "For when I am weak, then I am strong," from 2 Corinthians 12:10

Let go, to align with the Divine flow, and ignite your spirit. Do this and you'll find meaning in the miles. You'll run with so much enthusiasm that it takes you to the finish line, every time, all the time, in no time at all. It's here where running will feel like you're flowing downstream. You'll run faster, with less effort. However, it all starts with the act of allowing. Let go and feel the flow. As I like to say: I never race against another person, nor do I race against myself, *I let go*. I eliminate the resistance from within and allow my spirit to move me forward.

Remember this: living a life without struggle is an untrue promise. Our downfalls are life's most promising teachers. Yet living a life of peace is very possible. By learning the lesson, you accept the resistance, thus transcending the pain into a blissful experience.

2. Give a Consistent Effort to Increase Speed

A pheasant says to a bull, "I would love to get on top of that tree, but I haven't the energy."

"Well," says the bull, "why don't you eat some of my dung? It's packed with nutrients."

So the pheasant eats some dung and finds that it gives him enough energy to get to the first branch.

The next day, he eats some more and gets to the next branch. This cycle continues for a week.

Finally, the pheasant is at the top of the tree, where he is spotted by the farmer, who shoots him with a shotgun.

Moral of the story: bullsh*t might take you to the top, but it won't keep you there.

This old fable highlights a very profound principle learned through running. The principle is this: what you put into running, is what you get out of it. Putting in a diligent effort through training will prepare you for race day. Likewise, running without diligence may get you in trouble. This holds especially true when attempting to run a personal best. You may get out front early, only to crash and burn later.

Energy in is energy out. Taking each stride with intention is an honest way to run faster. You give everything. Not in a way where you crash and burn, surrendering to a DNF on race day. Instead, you can find real balance and journey steadily to the finish.

At this point, you may be thinking, "I get it, set an intention, but how do I determine the best pace?" Well, the answer is different for every runner. So feel it out. Don't forget, it's less about *force* and more about *alignment*. You are not *pushing* yourself to move, you are being *pulled* forward. You trade a run full of stress and force into one of harmony and flow.

Then comes the best news of all: by merely placing your focus on every step through training, you'll naturally become faster for race day. You don't have to clock times or keep track of your pace, either. I don't own a running watch. Keeping my mind off the clock and in the present moment has been a *huge* contribution to my progress. Plus, the less you rely on the numbers, the more sensitive you become to your speed. You can feel the difference between an edgy groove and a comfortable pace.

It also related to the awareness of negative self-talk. By focusing less on the external world of race splits, running gear, and supplements, you will have more time to listen to your inner world. You begin running from the inside-out rather than the outside-in. You then realize that inside is where the real power lies and where the infinite energy awaits. Eventually, you step back as the observer and view your thoughts subjectively. You snap out of unconscious doing.

Of course, you're going to have bad runs and good runs, but running mindfully guides focus to your inner world. You become honest with yourself. That is, you prevent excuses by not identifying with them. As a result, you see them for what they are—*excuses*—and let them go to run faster.

Never forget this: internal resistance will slow you down well before external resistance because you can see the separation between you and the resistance externally. It's easy to tell you're not the hill so you don't identify with it. However, internal resistance can be trickier. It feels like part of you and usually comes in the form of a self-limiting story.

That's why intending to take every step works so well. Even if you're feeling sluggish and are unable to run fast, you can still give focus. In this way, you run the best you can, changing your bad run into a good run every time. Don't we always run faster when having a good run?

3. Run in the Present Moment to Avoid Suffering

When running any length race, especially a new distance, if you get stuck in your thoughts, you're a slave to time. In other words, if you fixate on the finish line long enough, running feels like an eternity. 100-mile finishers surely know what I'm talking about. But it doesn't have to feel that way.

A mind stuck in the future creates an enormous amount of suffering. The longer the race, the deeper the grave you dig. Remember this: the thought of crossing the finish line while racing can create motivation, but obsessing over it can create anxiety. Fixating on the past can become problematic also.

Consider if you've taken a DNF in the past. The memory can inspire you to finish your next race. However, obsessing over it can create depression, sorrow, and despair. But remember, when you detach from your thoughts, they can become empowering. You can now leverage the past and future as motivation, instead of suffering from it.

So how does taking each step with intention help? By doing so, you are no longer obsessing over your past downfalls or potential future successes. By focusing on each step, you are able to let go of your thoughts and find the present moment. Still, if self-sabotaging thoughts arise, acknowledge them without judgment, and let them pass. Afterward, bring your focus back to each step at hand.

Also, understand that *visualizing* crossing the finish line and *obsessing* over it are different. The practice of visualization can create success. The habit of clinging to thoughts can create suffering. Visualize the finish line in training, but forget it on race day. The course is the course, the distance is laid out. So adjust your focus. Don't count the miles, count your blessings. This is an approach you can always count on.

4. Transcend Pain to Prevent Slowing Down

Running with intention produces an edgy groove. This keeps you at the near breaking point of your pain threshold. Any faster and you may blow a gasket; back off and you may lose momentum. It's tempting to focus less to find more comfort in a sport that makes you so uncomfortable, but don't. Instead of avoiding the pain, transform and absorb it.

How does one make this happen? Or better yet, how does one *allow* this to happen? The answer lies in your mind. No, I'm not delivering a magic pill here, but that doesn't make it any less magical. What you're about to learn is how to transcend the pain of every step no matter the pain level. It's through the power of *gratitude.*

As I like to say, when you're grateful, it's impossible to feel bad, and in a sport where discomfort is a guarantee, gratitude will help you along the way. As human beings, for whatever reason, we see sacrifice as a way to give back. A way to show an appreciation for life. Although this is a mental position in the mind, still, we give ourselves, whether that's through hard work or going above and beyond for others. If anything, it provides balance back to our unbalanced and often stressful lives.

By giving yourself, you are allowing grace to flow into your life, creating an opening. It's in giving that we receive. The true giving-receiving relationship is about circulation, not transaction. It's like blood flow. Allowing both sides to take place creates a healthy circulation, thus creating a healthy body and mind. Only receiving or only giving stops the flow, like a clot, creating dis-ease. If this thought resonates with you, then let running become a thank-you for the gift of life. Give thanks.

Every step of appreciation can transcend the pain, but it takes honesty. No one is watching you run. You must be honest with yourself. You'll know if you stay on an edgy groove or not. Even with a crowded mind, once you run into the stillness, you'll know. Gratitude is not some new thought or idea. It's been practiced for thousands of years.

So intend to take every step and accept the suffering. Don't avoid it. It's in the pain where you will learn your greatest lessons. Then, when you're ready, transcend it by giving thanks. Allow it to transcend into a new dimension, and when the fireworks begin to go off on the screen of your mind—you'll understand this better when it occurs—you'll become inspired (in spirit). Suddenly, you're no longer running alone, you're running from a greater whole. You go from running to flying, letting go, soaring through every mile. Now give focus, give thanks, and never give up!

5. Detach From the Ego to Avoid Burnout

While racing, there will be times you'll want to increase your pace. Especially when you start feeling faster, quicker, and lighter on your feet after following the advice of this book. Any time this occurs, I remind myself to relax and trust the process. I tell myself to fall back into that edgy groove. No matter who is ahead or behind me, I get back to focusing on each stride. That's it.

Not only does this prevent burnout or a sluggish pace, it helps you detach from the highs and lows that come with any ultramarathon. By doing so, you significantly reduce the chances of a DNF. In this way, you're no longer a victim of your circumstances, but instead, the creator. Now you have control of your run—and race—finishing with the best outcome based on your current stamina.

The key is to detach from your outer runner, and let your inner runner free. Running while motivated by external reward only takes us so far. In this way, you are running from an egoic state. You are running from the "outer runner."

Your outer runner is motivated by things like finisher medals, online race times, and finish line photos. Although there's nothing wrong with using these outcomes to progress, you may find them to be short-lived. Running with this mindset will shorten longevity and become problematic. You'll notice the longer you run, the more difficult it becomes for your outer runner to keep up.

So unless you discover a deeper meaning in the distance, it becomes relatively easy to give up on ultra running—or ultra running will give up on you. That's because external rewards come and go, and although they provide a sense of satisfaction in the moment, they are empty in nature. On the other hand, if you look inward for motivation, you'll find it to be everlasting. The depths of your inner dwelling stretch far beyond what we could ever comprehend.

When you find a deeper meaning in your running, you'll also find a deeper understanding of your inner runner. Your outer runner creates limitations; your inner runner surpasses them. Run from the inside-out and trust the process. This is the core message of running faster mindfully.

6. Run While Fasting to Run Forever

There are unbelievable powers that arise from fasting. In fact, fasting is a common practice in many cultures. The benefits are remarkable. Deep cleansing, enhanced intuition, and a fat-adapted body are only the start. Personally, as I've shared before, I routinely run 50K with no food or water. I also run at least the first 20 miles of any distance on empty. Something about running 100 miles only with fluids feels refreshing. It's a humbling experience.

I provided instructions on fasting and running in the previous chapter. However, I thought it would be helpful to expand on it for running faster as I believe fat adaptation is the foundation for running faster mindfully.

To help, when running on empty, if I'm thirsty, I ask myself these words: Am I suffering yet? If the answer is no, I then refrain from consumption. For me, eating food during a run, especially on race day, provides too much comfort. When this occurs, the run loses its magic. I lose grace in my pace. Once the struggle becomes too demanding, I step away from exclusion and replace it with inclusion. It's a wedge between the ego and self. Here's where you detach from self-sabotaging thoughts on race day. How could you ever fatigue with life energy flowing in you and all around you? Liveliness replaces tiredness, and ultra running becomes less exhausting.

Sometimes we have to *not* perform as we usually do to break free of our old ways. It's not that you don't do anything at all, it's just that any doing becomes nonreactive. You yield to overcome, breaking free of compulsive cycles, thus regaining consciousness and getting into a position where change become a real possibility.

At times, we need to fail instead of succeed. Lose instead of win. Let go instead of hold on. Sometimes it takes being cold, tired, and weak to find our true strength because it's in our emptiness where we find fullness. You must lose yourself before you can find yourself. We trek down our path, in this journey of life, lost, only to find our way home later and rediscover who we are, experiencing ourselves again for the first time.

When I'm running in a fasted state, it's much easier to surrender and align with the flow of life, with spirit, with oneness. Fasting empties out the negativity making way for positivity. The light can't enter without the cracks of a broken shell. Plus, fasting while running helps *enormously* with becoming fat-adapted, as fat adaptation allows you to tap into a near-infinite supply of energy from within. That energy is fat, and through fat-adapted running, you'll run longer with what feels like less effort.

Body fat is actually a wonderful thing. It's potential energy. It's an adaptation over thousands of years of feast and famine. Fasting and eating naturally will bring you back to your roots and to this available energy. Plus, your body will feel amazing.

It's also important to note that becoming fat-adapted doesn't mean you run without sugar. Instead, you develop a base. You consume less sugar because your body is much more efficient at burning its own fat as fuel. Running on low sugar can significantly reduce stomach issues in longer races such as 100- and 200-mile distances (at least it has for me).

As a fat-adapted runner, you become less reliant on external sources of energy. You have more available energy from within, making the distance between aid stations almost irrelevant. Plus, running fasted allows for much more clarity and insight. You start developing meaning in your running. As a result, you will build an unstoppable mindset and a frame of mind that will carry you through the lowest of lows of an ultramarathon. That, or you will find yourself detached from the ups and downs completely. If fat adaptation is a new concept for you, consider the snake in the dark room:

Close your eyes and imagine you are sitting in a dark room. There's no way out. The room is silent when, without warning, a voice comes over a loudspeaker. It tells you this: there's a big deadly snake in the room! You feel a rush of fear shoot up your spine, knowing the snake can bite you at any moment.

Suddenly, across the room, you see a big dark figure. It's the snake! Adrenaline pumps through your veins and just when you're about to lose it, a flash of light illuminates the room—*flash*. What looked like a snake was actually a big rope. Within a split second, your fear vanishes. Gone completely. Although the light was only momentary, it gave you a glimpse of truth. Your experience in the room will never be the same again.

In this example, the room is your running, and fat adaptation is the snake. Letting go of outdated practices like carbo-loading can be scary. I know, I've been there myself. However, once you see the truth, meaning, once you finish that first run as a fat-adapted runner without feeling sluggish, you get a keener insight. You realize anyone can run any ultra distance, and fat adaptation is most definitely the way to go.

Fast Mindful Ultramarathon Running

If you've ever wondered how to run faster without the added stress of competition and expectations, now you know. As you've now learned, running faster isn't solely for competitors. In fact, increasing speed can very well be for anyone, including you.

If you direct your focus in the right direction, the possibilities are endless. By taking each step with intention, you'll run faster progressively and get the most out of each run. As a result, you have a better chance of reaching a personal best.

Running faster mindfully doesn't require a watch, and you surely don't need to track your pace or heart rate. No more worries about placement, and because of this change in attitude, race-day anxiety will be dramatically reduced. So focus on your footsteps, stay in the present moment, and enjoy the journey along the way.

Finally, let's head over to the final chapter of *Mindful Ultramarathon Running* where I offer the greatest gift of all.

CONCLUSION:

The Gift

The moment you choose a mindful approach to ultramarathon running is the moment your life begins to change. One day you strive, and the next day, you arrive. You fall asleep to a form of running where you push to the finish line with hunger, determination, and grit. You'll wake up to a new world where force transcends to flow, from form to formless. No longer are you pushing forward, as you now feel pulled by a greater power. Instead of hunger, that is, feeling a lack, you feel whole and abundant. You don't strain to gain, you find a groove and simply move.

Mindful ultramarathon running sure comes with many magnificent benefits. Yet maybe the most beneficial one of all is how to handle pain. Meaning, how well you deal with suffering. Because here's the secret: inside suffering awaits a very special gift that can alter the entire course of your life in a moment.

What's this gift I speak of? I will explain shortly, but first, allow me to tell the story of how I came to this realization. It involves the day I "woke up," the day running transformed my life forever. The story starts on marathon race day . . .

"My name is Michael D'Aulerio! My name is Michael D'Aulerio!" Screaming this phrase at the top of my lungs was far from helpful as my identity began slipping away. I stagger-stepped to the side of the road.

Race-day determination began transforming into confusion and fear. Every step forward was one step closer to complete and utter insanity. Until finally it hit! The worse got even worse; I completely forgot who I was.

I remember thinking to myself, "Is this how the sick feel?" "Is this how the insane feel?" "Is this how it feels to have dementia?" I was far into a marathon, and something beyond hitting the wall occurred. As I wandered off to the side of the road, I had zero recollection of who I was or what I was doing. I felt lost, lost for words, lost for direction, and lost for reality. When I glanced up at a billboard, the words on the advertisement looked like symbols of some sort. The same symbols appeared on my GPS watch. As I heard the spectators of the marathon beside me, it sounded like they were speaking in gibberish.

Then it happened. I began feeling a warm and dense paralyzing rush through my body. It started down at my feet and began working its way up. First, my legs felt paralyzed, slowly forcing me to the ground. As the feeling rose up my body, I began to lose it! The paralyzing rush then started working its way up through my torso, forcing my body to the ground. At this point, I could only move my neck.

I raised my head, looking down at my body as I began to develop panicking thoughts. "What is happening to me?" "Why am I losing control of my body?" and "Who the hell am I?" Hundreds of similar questions were racing through my mind at once. As the warm wave of numbness began to reach my neck, I had no idea what was happening, who I was, or what to do. My neck control was now gone, and I was lying flat on the ground with zero mobility.

When I was at the tipping point of losing any physiological stability I had left, suddenly, it happened. Suddenly, feeling almost faithful, I knew what to do. The moment when your legs give up is the exact moment when your heart gives more. My heart, subconscious mind, spirit—whatever you'd like to call it—knew exactly what to do.

In the moment of nothingness, I began developing images of bright lights. My natural instinct was to picture bright lights and to have a positive state of mind. You know those positive thoughts where you develop a tingling rush phenomenon? Like an emotional sensation gained from achieving something great? Or the feeling you get from a beautiful piece of music?

With zero idea of who I was, somehow, I knew entering into a positive state of being was the key to reversing the effect. A natural instinct, perhaps, or possibly a deep-seated knowing likely developed from a decade of reading books on health, spirituality, and personal development.

Anyway, I closed my eyes and began taking deep breaths of fresh air while visualizing big bright lights in the sky. The flashes of light got brighter and brighter until, out of nowhere, it happened: *flash*—a complete whiteout.

It felt as if I had been struck by a grand luminescent light. A radiance far past anything I could ever envision. It was not forceful, I didn't produce the light, but instead, it felt as if I let it in because of being in such a broken-down and vulnerable state. The light's radiance penetrated my entire body. It was timeless, surreal, and peaceful. In an instant, my fear and anxiety vanished. I was no longer scared or lonely. I felt healed and whole.

At the time I had no interest in what transpired. I was just grateful. I thought to myself, "It worked," and the paralyzing rush began making its way in the opposite direction. As the feeling began leaving my body, I started remembering who I was. It was the greatest relief of my life!

After spending some time collecting my thoughts, reality began making its way back. My identity returned! "Wait, I'm a runner and I'm on the sidelines of some sort of race. Hold on, am I running a marathon? Yes, I'm running a marathon!" I picked myself up with my naturally determined mindset and began moving forward.

With no idea what mile I was on, I began walking. This movement was an unusual feeling. It felt like I had rubber legs on a sheet of ice. There was something off about the connection between my brain to my feet. But it didn't matter; quitting was not an option. I kept moving forward. I pulled myself together and somehow crossed the finish line.

Something happened that day, something that changed my running forever, and my life. At the height of my breakdown, what could have seemed like uncontrollable stress felt more like a feeling of intense calmness. First, it was suffering, and then, a state of presence. It felt peaceful beyond words and developed an extraordinary sense of oneness, of infinite love, a feeling that hasn't left since. There was no start or finish. It was an illumination. I was no longer my body, but the conscious awareness, a state beyond any description, beyond any time.

Later that day, I vomited profusely and had an elevated heart rate for days. For weeks I could not concentrate. I didn't discuss this experience with anyone. Plus, I was likely living from a lower vibration. A place where I could not find appreciation in what exactly transpired. The experience was something beyond the physical, beyond my senses, and beyond time.

The person I was died that day. I felt reborn. I woke up and broke free from a life of amnesia. I could not help but see our existence from a greatly expanded perspective. "I" and "myself" were now distinctly separate. I was not my thoughts nor the thinker. I was the observer, that is, I was purely conscious. It was a spiritual awakening.

I became much more sensitive to energy and now live with a strong sense of togetherness. This is not something to debate or describe, it's not a what, but an *is*-ness, a *being*-ness. For the first time, I understood what it was to *be* a human *being*. Although I still own material objects, I no longer feel an attachment to them. No longer do I feel pain losing or not obtaining something physical. Instead, at times, I feel pain from the attachment to it, and either suffer willingly or let it go.

That also goes for the mind as well. When you detach from the mind, you find your true strength. By breaking free from compulsive thinking, you realize how powerful this tool can be. Now, *impossible* is only a word to describe the unknown territory that sits on the other side of what your mind considers possible. Detach from the mind, and there are no limitations.

Regardless of what occurred that day, a few months later, I found myself at the starting line of my next marathon. But something was different this time around. When I crossed the finish line, I felt like I could endure much more. Why could I run more? Isn't 26.2 miles the limit?

After the race, I went back to tell the man who had introduced me to distance running in the first place. The man who saw something in me and inspired me to run marathons. He began to tell me stories about the world of ultra running. He spoke stories of some of the greatest distance runners on planet earth. People who ran across the United States and the Sahara Desert. A man who ran 300 plus straight miles without stopping. Runners who shatter twenty-four-hour running records, who run for six days, and compete in 100-mile mountain races in the sky. A group of athletes who live outside the realm of athletics.

It didn't make sense to me at the time. How had I never heard of these extraordinary athletes? Instead of being doubtful or confused about the thought, I began to get excited! I took a long deep breath, and oddly enough, it felt like home. And this was the day I became an ultramarathon runner in my heart.

Within the next few years, between races and training runs, I completed over 100 ultra distances. I've run 50Ks, 50 miles, 100Ks, 100 miles, 200 miles, and longer. I've run 60-mile training runs, over twenty-four hours straight, and 116 miles across the state of Florida. I went from barely finishing a marathon and feeling like a truck hit me, to running 100-mile ultramarathons with incredible strength.

Sure, running these distances may look like some great achievement from the outside. But the truth is, deep down, that was never my focus. The distance I travel outwardly is merely a reflection of the distance I travel inwardly. Each race has been a marker of my inner journey.

Now, here's the gift . . .

What you'll receive from mindful ultramarathon running is an *awakening*. You learn how to transcend suffering both inside and outside your running shoes. As there are two ways to experience an awakening through ultra running:

1. Suffer so much from the mileage that you surrender because you can't take the pain anymore. Eventually, over the distance, your mind breaks, causing a detachment, and an awakening into a new life. Unfortunately, there's no way of knowing how long this will take. Whether it's a few races, a few years, or a few decades.

OR

2. Choose the path consciously. Through mindful ultramarathon running, you learn to let go of your attachment to time. No more focusing on the past and future while running; instead, you run from timelessness, a place where it's nonexistent, a place to call home.

How does "waking up" help with the pain and suffering of ultramarathon running and life? Well, pain and time are inseparable. So you find a peaceful life in the NOW, instead of a stressful one in the past or future. You choose no more pain, no more suffering, and run ultra distances from a place of no time, in no time at all.

Ultramarathon running is much like life. You'll experience good days and bad days, highs and lows, slow time and fast times, but you only have one journey, *your* journey, and what a beautiful struggle that path can be.

Where the Path Leads

As a writer and a human being, I felt guided to write this book. There was something that consumed me, and wouldn't stop until the words transferred onto the page. You may feel the same about a future race. I know I did when it came to my first ultramarathon, and the first time I ran 100 and 200 miles. Once it entered into my consciousness, it was unshakable. I didn't have a choice. Either I made it through training and across the finish line, or I dealt with constant regret.

If you feel the same about your first or next ultramarathon, on a deeper level, you likely have a lesson to learn. Maybe it's to discover something new about yourself from the suffering. Or to become stronger, wiser, and more enduring. Or perhaps it's to practice the way of a mindful ultramarathon runner, to wake up, and see life from a new light. It may be time to heal, or to heal someone you love greatly.

Naturally, self-doubt will appear, but just like weeds arise in every garden, opposing forces come with any new challenge. I've had the pleasure to serve many runners in their path to reaching new distances, and there's one common theme I've found. The theme is this: everyone is capable of running faster, longer, and stronger. Period.

You will find your way. Let go. Run from the limitlessness that is your being. Do this, and the finish line will come. If you continue to move your feet forward, in the present moment, you will arrive. It's where you'll become the alchemist of your experience. But instead of turning copper into gold, pain turns into joy, struggle into love, and suffering into bliss.

Before, when you gazed up at the moon during an ultramarathon, you possibly felt a longing, a sense of loneliness. Now, when you're out running into the night, when your legs are broken, chafing for hours, with a nauseated stomach, and a heavy dose of exhaustion, you will look up at the same moon. But now, it seems much different through your new eyes, the eyes of a mindful ultramarathon runner.

No longer do you feel lonely. You now have a sense of togetherness, of hope, and of adventure. You no longer feel separate from anything. The wholeness is infinite, it's eternal, it's *love*. When you run from this limitless space, there are no boundaries or obstacles. All you need to do is allow the power of love to flow. Remember, we don't push ourselves into love, we fall in love, and to fall, you must do what? Yes, that's right: you must *let go*.

Now stresses won't magnify over the miles. Every act of forgiveness breaks one chain holding you back from reaching your greatness. Forgive others, and yourself, because love is immeasurable. When you release the burdens, you let your natural energy flow freely, and now, running an ultramarathon becomes a joyful experience.

When you enter into the invisible realm of love, limitations are nonexistent. You fall asleep to the impossible and wake up to what's really possible: anything you surrender to and let naturally flow into your life.

You are now on the mindful ultramarathon running path, and that path is *love*.

Welcome home.

My forward motion is diligent because your love is forever. In this way, how could I ever give up?

Printed in Great Britain
by Amazon

37054242R00076